THIS ISLE OF GUEMES

by

HELEN TROY ELMORE

GUEMES ISLAND, WASHINGTON

HELEN TROY ELMORE

Helen Troy Elmore was born in Colorado but grew up in the town of Colfax in eastern Washington. While still a young woman she moved to Hawaii, where she met her husband. During the years she lived there she wrote poetry and short stories, as well as a column for the Maui News on the island of Maui. Mrs. Elmore has traveled extensively all over the world and has lived in various parts of Europe. She now resides on the island of Guemes.

Besides *This Isle of Guemes*, the author has to her credit *Dust Before the Wind*, telling a portion of the history of World War Two in the Hawaiian Islands (selections from the book are now in the Archives of Hawaii), and *Hold Me Forever*, in which she tells of her life in Hawaii.

This Isle of Guemes was originally published in 1973 by Helen Troy Elmore and sponsored by the Community Club of Guemes Island.
Cover illustration by by Helen Troy Elmore.

Guemes Gleanings was published in 1981 by Gertrude Howard as an "unduplicated continuation of... *This Isle of Guemes*."

ISBN: 978-1460905708

2011 reprint sponsored by LineTime.org

Dedicated to those who first
knew Guemes—the Indian
people and the pioneers.

To Guemes—

How still the wood
Beneath the winter snow—
How soft the footstep
of the buck and doe—
Nature sleeps,
Knowing the waiting heart
of Spring—
And soon, within the wood
A bird will sing.

FOREWORD

TWO RESIDENTS of Guemes Island, Mrs. Gertie Howard and Mrs. Meta Whicker, have, for a number of years, collected information pertaining to the island's past. They have gathered old letters, statements from descendants of pioneers, old newspapers and records, often scribbled in pencil, of community affairs of business, family and social significance. They have done this with the hope that all of the material may be brought together in a book, a book which will become a part of the available and concentrated history of the San Juan Islands of Washington State.

Memories of a few Guemes residents of the present have been included in this book, in addition to the collection of Mrs. Howard and Mrs. Whicker. The contents do not present precise historic detail but rather an over all portrayal of what Guemes has been from the time the first people came and called it home.

Many quotations from tangible material are copied in original form in the book's content in the belief that the written and spoken word should be presented as it has been preserved—as a portion of the chronography of the Island.

Dedicated to those who first knew Guemes—the Indian people and the pioneers.

Aside from those named in the pages which follow, surely there have been others whose lives are not recorded but who, in their way and in their time, gave something of value which contributes silently with meaning, to those who live upon Guemes, today.

This book has been written, not by a long time resident of the island, but by one who is, rather, a recent comer who has been drawn to this place because of the charm of its simplicity and because of its people. Drawn, too, by the colorful and interesting background of this minute world, reaching above the inlets of Puget Sound.

CHAPTER ONE

SOMEWHERE, WITHIN the great miracle of creation, the San Juan islands of the American Northwest came into being.

In the beginning, the islands appeared as barren rocky summits above the surface of seemingly endless water. There were many of these islands, some large, some small, and they lay lone and still under the heat of summer sun and the battering strength of a winter sea.

Lone and still they lay—and milleniums passed.

But the San juans were not to be forever barren and alone. From the deep, unfathomable mystery of life came transfiguration. upon these islands soil formed, roots found the soil and took hold until trees were there, reaching toward the sky, grasses enriched the meadows, flowers bloomed. Wildlife came in many forms, changing as environment demanded. Birds sang from branches of deep forest growth. Furry animals grazed upon the green of the land. Water fowl swam near island shores and ate fish from the ocean depth.

One day, man walked from an ancient world of the east across a narrow strip of land to become known as Bering Strait. He walked and found the many islands, now the San Juans, and he saw them and the big continent beyond them as a place he wished to live. Generations later his descendants would be known as the "Red Men," the North American Indians.

After an interval in time, other men arrived. They came from afar in ships under sail, blown by the varied winds to anchorage off shore near the San Juans. This was a new world for these men, different from Spain, from England, from the east coast of North. America and the parts of the globe from which they came to explore.

From the deck of the "Discovery," its British flag waving overhead, the master of the barque, Captain Vancouver, saw the waters of the Pacific reaching along the coastline, into the many inlets, washing myriad island beaches and rugged cliffs and he named this endless surge of the sea "Puget Sound." Thus he honored one of his lieutenants who served him well.

Captain Vancouver sent his men out from his fleet in small boats and, as they located various islands, he named them after certain members of his crew—Blakely—Whidby and others. Spanish explorers followed a like pattern and one of them, Eliza, in 1792, named the whole group of islands he had seen "Isla y Archipelago de San Juan." On one of his ventures away from his mother ship, Eliza, the Spanish captain, came ashore on a small island. There it was, emerald green, between two waterways, now Bellingham and Guemes Channels, inlets, as Vancouver called them. Captain Eliza thought of the man who had sent him to the high seas to seek and to find. This man was the Viceroy of Mexico. His name was "Senor Don Juan Vicente de Gueme Pacheco y Padilla Oreasites y Aguayo, Conde de Revilla Gigedo." From this lengthy title, Eliza chose the name "Gueme" for the small terrain upon which he stood. "Guemes" it became to those who later inhabited it, although, for a time, the name "Lawrence Island" was used. Then "Guemes" was rewritten on the charts and Captain Eliza's choice has been perpetuated.

The early explorers found Indian people or signs of their

previous encampment on the many islands of the San juans which they visited. It has been said that no tribe lived permanently upon the island of Guemes. However, in his book, "Indians of Skagit County," recently published, Chief Martin J. Sampson states "The Samish tribe, in 1855 owned Guemes, Samish, Cypress, Lopez and the western half of Fidalgo island," though, he says, they occupied only Guemes and Samish islands permanently. Chief Sampson acknowledges that anthropologists have designated all of the Skagit tribes as Salish but he believes that the Guemes and Lummi tribes are related and that much of their language was not understood by the Salish nor was it a part of the Salish language and that the Guemes and Lummi Indians, though akin to the coastal division of the Salish, were more Samish than Salish.

A sketch of archeological sites from University of Washington files shows four sites of Indian occupation on Guemes. Two are on the west coast, one on the east, a little to the north, and one on the south coast. Middens have been found on all sites but the area midway along the west shore, now known as Potlatch Beach, seems to have been the main gathering and dwelling place of Guemes Indians. There, close to the waters of Bellingham channel, a few years ago, the remains of an Indian longhouse were removed. Chief Sampson, in his book, mentions this house. Island residents of today have photographs of small Indian dwellings on the slope of the hill above the place where the longhouse once stood. A gnarled old apple tree still bears its fruit near the clear waters of a spring and people who live on Guemes say: "The Indian tribe who once lived here planted that tree!"

It is regrettable that the longhouse on Guemes, the scene of potlatches, was allowed to disintegrate. Through many years it was neglected though it was a fine example of a certain type of longhouse, having partitions which made separate rooms for different visiting tribes when they came as guests for a potlatch celebration. As late as 1917, Shelton saw the house and wrote that it was "full of people." Chief Sampson tells us that the last potlatch on Guemes was held in the 1880s and a clipping from an old Anacortes, Washington, newspaper dated January 19, 1884, reads— "Great numbers of canoes containing entire families of Indians, the women and girls dressed in the brightest colors, passed Anacortes on Tuesday, on their way home from the potlatch held at their rendezvous on Guemes Island." To that festivity, —delegates came from all tribes on Puget Sound, even from Vancouver Island and the Fraser River area.

According to historians who have written of the Indians of the American Northwest, some of them writers among the Indian race themselves, the word "Potlatch" means, in a broad sense, "to give." Certain authorities say it comes from the Chinook, a jargon of many Indian tongues which enabled various tribes to converse when trading even though they were unfamiliar with one another's established dialects. Others believe it evolved from the Nootka verb "Pa-chitle," to give. Whichever derivation and choice the meaning of potlatch remains the same.

During the potlatches on Guemes, as elsewhere, gifts were given and received. There was feasting, dancing, singing, and there were speeches. Also, the host often honored his guests by singing his own song. This was considered a presentation of merit. Any Indian who gave a potlatch attained prestige among all tribes.

Certain Puget Sound Indian tribes are said to have been warlike. The Haidas, Tsmichians and Makahs, came sometimes to the south and made surprise raids on other Indians, killing some, taking others home with them to use as slaves.

Explorers, however, found most of the Indian people they encountered to be friendly, even generous with their offerings of 'fish or meat from the hunt. With few exceptions no harm came to the early explorers and reports of Indian attack upon white people came after the breaking of promises to the Indians or mistreatment of them.

The Indians of Guemes Island have a peaceful history. They built their village by the side of "the big water." There were differences in tribal customs but they were insignificant and the way of life on Guemes Island for the Indians who lived here was basically similar to that of other coastal people of their race.

As we refer to those Indians who came to Guemes to make their home, the physical and spiritual aspects of these individuals come into focus.

They were stalwart with heavy bodies and broad faces, with prominent cheek bones. Proportionately to the general build, their legs are said to have been less developed.

The words of a long gone American poet could well have been written for the Indian. William Cullen Bryant, into whose own life Nature entered, revealed his recognition and his understanding in "Thanatopsis" —The Indian who, as a part of his spiritual life, had listened to Nature so long before, had he read this poem, could he have read it, would have grasped within a moment, its meaning. The first few lines of "Thanatopsis" are enough—

> "To him who in the love of Nature holds
> Communion with her visible forms, she speaks
> A various language."

To the Guemes Indian people, along with countless of their race, Nature spoke. They lived, a part of her. For them each form on earth, in sky, in water, had a spirit. Every,, tree, every flower, animal and bird had a soul. Mountains, rivers, the sea, all communed with these people with clear voice and vibrant meaning.

To those who reach, toward Nature in our world, this spiritual faith of the Indian is a thing of beauty. It is a different approach from many beliefs of the white man but none the less acceptable as one searches the depths of the fullness of Life, itself.

The Indian stood beneath a great and spreading tree and felt an inaudible word, a whisper of truth. Nature's eloquent quietude, even her wildest moments of storm, strengthened him and gave him his great love for the world in which it was his destiny to live.

The Indian was taught he must acquire a second spirit, one associated with his physical being, one which would be with him each moment of his life. He must earn this spirit in accordance with his tribal belief through sacrifice, through deprivation during a period of his youth. When he had suffered enough, his spirit would make his power felt, and once the Indian became aware of this, the spirit remained the influence concerning his every word and, deed and guided the way of the Indian as he walked his earthly years.

So it was. The Guemes Indians lived in harmony with the cardinal beliefs and customs of their race.

Indian dwellings in permanent villages such as the one on Guemes, were fashioned of split cedar lumber. Indians made their tools of wood and of stone. Canoes carved from the log of the cedar were seaworthy. Knives were carved from bones and horns of animals and bark scraped from the valuable cedar tree was beaten into a fibre which was used for weaving mats and other articles, even for wearing apparel, as a substitute for cloth.

Archie Binn, in his book "Sea in the Forest," tells us that

after the first Asians came and settled in the American Northwest others arrived bringing dogs "with fleece as thick as wool
of sheep." We hear, even today, often, of such dogs having been
with the Guemes Indians in their village and in their canoes as
they rode the waters of Puget Sound. Early explorers, Vancouver included, wrote of having seen these dogs and thought they
resembled somewhat the sled dogs of Russia. The Guemes Indians sheared their dogs and used the heavy coats for the weaving
of blankets and also for some of their own clothing. Because of
the presence of many of these animals Guemes was sometimes
referred to as "Dog Island."

There was no need for hunger among the Indians here, on
Guemes. It was a matter of diligence and the knowledge and
intuition, so existent among primitive people, as to which of
Nature's offerings were edible and how to prepare them for
immediate consumption and, too, for preservation.

The blue of the Camas flower colored certain areas of Guemes
and the Indians savored its bulb-like root for food. It was, to
them, a delicacy and no one of another tribe was welcome to
it where it grew on what the Guemes Indians considered their
territory. Several kinds of berries were available—salal, salmon-
berry, raspberry and blackberry—all grew on Guemes and were
gathered in season to be eaten fresh or dried. Acorns and hazel-
nuts were here too. The cattail, the fern, the dandelion, even the
nettle, all were part of Indian food—that which came from the
land, and all of this, together with clams and fish from the sea,
with its oil content, brought a rounded well balanced diet.

Fish was often traded for meat with Indian tribes who, living
east of the Cascades, had no contact with ocean waters and
hunted forest animals for their food. Deer, bear, elk, wildcat, all
were sought by these hunting tribes.

It was not customary among Indian people to kill animals for sport or pleasure. They killed for meat, for food, and for skins for warmth and for their own garments. Indians respected their kill and wasted no part of it because the life of the animal had been sacrificed for their own preservation.

Filial loyalty, as a characteristic of the Indian, has been revealed. On one occasion a young girl belonging to the Guemes tribe had an offer of marriage from a white man she loved.

"My mother is old and sick," she told him. "I cannot marry so long as she lives. I must care for her every day, every night."

The man waited. But the young girl died as the mother lived on.

Today there is no Indian village along Potlatch Beach on the western shore of the island of Guemes. The village is long gone. It is gone the way of all Indian tribal settlements of our land. Camping localities, where middens are found, have not heard for many a year, the sound of Indian voices or Indian laughter. A few Indian families live on Guemes, some of them descendants of the Salish and Samish tribes. They live-quiet, respected citizens in their comfortable island homes. But, surely, they know the echo of their Indian past as they walk along the beaches of Guemes, even as they drive their modern automobiles along the country roads which once were paths trodden by the mocassined feet of their forefathers.

There is an Indian burial ground on Guemes Island.

Chief Seattle, of the Salishan blood, chief of the Duwamish tribe, upon surrendering his land to Governor Isaac Stevens in the year 1855-uttered these words,

"To us, the ashes of our ancestors are sacred and their resting place is hallowed ground."

Sadly enough, the graves of the Indians on Guemes have been desecrated, some of them, by those who are not Indian, by those who listened not to the words of Seattle, the Northwest Indian Chief.

But now, Nature with her strong and persistent force, has moved to protect the hallowed Indian ground. The forest has hidden it from the covetous glance of mankind. Birds sing in the tree tops above the graves and build their nests among spreading branches which shadow the earth beneath. Deer walk softly upon secret paths to lie and sleep upon the long grass covering the resting place of a people who once lived in concord with all growing things of earth.

This hallowed place lies at last, unseen, unfound, untouched by human hand.

The great Chief Joseph of the Nez Perce nation went before the Government of the United States to plead, not only for his own tribes but for his people everywhere, the

Guemes Indians included. His words are imprinted indelibly upon the pages of American history.

"The earth was created by the assistance of the sun and it should be left as it was. The country was made without line of demarcation and it is no man's business to divide it.... I see the whites all over the country gaining wealth and see their desire to give us lands which are worthless.... The earth and myself are of one mind. The measure of the land and the measure of our bodies are the same. Say to us, if you can say it, that you were sent by the Creative Power to talk to us. Perhaps you think the Creator sent you here to dispose of us as you see fit. If I thought you were sent by the Creator I might be induced to think you had a right to dispose of me. Do not misunderstand me, but understand me fully with reference to my affection for the land. I never said the land was mine to do with it as I chose. The one who has the right to dispose of it is the one who created it. I claim a right to live on my land and accord you the privilege to live on yours."

And, with the great gift of poetic expression, so prevalent in Indian oratory, Crowfoot, spokesman for the Blackfoot Confederacy, whispered during his last hour—

"What is Life? It is the flash of a firefly in the night. It is the breath of a buffalo in the winter time. It is the little shadow which runs across the grass and loses itself in the sunset."

CHAPTER TWO

THAT PLACE, where earth and sky seem to meet, has, from a remote past, caused man to pause and to wonder.

"What lies beyond?" he has whispered to himself, "What new world may be there, to see?"

This wondering, then, became a dream. And, to make the dream come true, man forsook a familiar place, an accepted mode of life, no matter where. Across uncharted seas, he sailed in small ships bruised by wind and water—over the lonely prairie and towering mountains—across wide and raging rivers of continents of which he knew only with the passage of each ensuing day, as he went his way.

It was inevitable that be learned that no matter how steadily and how long he journeyed, as he looked ahead, there was always that place where earth and sky seemed to meet. There was always the horizon.

Learning this, man began to turn his glance this direction and that and it came to him he had found already something of what lay beyond the past he had known. There were similarities and differences which, in thought, he compared to his former environment, wherever it may have been, but there was a freshness in this new country, a freshness and a serenity untrodden and unspoiled.

Now, man, as he journeyed, began to think of ceasing his

search, which could never end beyond the horizon, to choose a bit of earth for his own. Some of these wayfarers chose a valley-others a mountain slope, a river bank or a wooded grove. But, as they reached the Northwest of America, close to the great waters of the Pacific, they saw its arms reach inward. There was the continent and there were, too, small areas of land which separated one from another, lay in sea channels, in mystery and in beauty. Islands, each a diminutive world where lived tribes of Indian people, birds of the air and animals of the forest.

Some of the travelers ceased their journeying and chose to live upon an island. Some of them chose Guemes.

Reputedly, a man named Hall was the island~s first white settler. He built a small house on the south shore but after a short stay, his dream apparently unfulfilled, he went away, no one knows why. However, soon after his departure others came, one of whom, in 1871, was Bill Payne. He was the son of Irish parents who had migrated to America. As a young restless boy, Bill, too, had seen a horizon. He crossed the plains with a party of Mormons. After some prospecting and a time in the Klondike, Bill Payne settled on Guemes and lived upon the island for close to half a century. On his 75th birthday he reminisced, portraying his long years to a representative of the Anacortes American, a newspaper published on Fidalgo Island, across the channel from Guemes.

He recalled that a man named Kittle came to the island about the time, though a little later, than Hall had arrived. Mr. Payne cited a number of people who were settlers before 1871—James Matthews, H. P. O'Bryant, William Whaley, Pat Mahoney, John MacKintosh, Sol and John Shriver. In February, 1872, John Edens, later to become a senator, arrived and after him Porter, Henry and Bill Edens all took claims on Guemes. Amos

Johnson and a Mr. Nicholas came and in the same year Lucius Blackinton became a resident of the island.

It has been possible to acquire detailed information concerning a few of the above mentioned pioneers.

Humphrey Posey O'Bryant was born in Georgia March 28, 1828, son of Duncan and Martha (Whitehead) O'Bryant.

In March, 1843, he crossed the plains with a company of 575 persons, arriving in October of that year. He worked on the first house built in Portland, Oregon, and hewed logs for the first warehouse there. In 1847 he went to California and was a member of one of the parties to work in the mines. He returned to Portland in 1849 and in'1853 he went to Olympia, Washington, and was subsequently appointed by Governor Stevens as Indian agent at Port Madison. Mr. O'Bryant was active in the Indian wars in California, Oregon and Washington. On April 12, 1866, he settled on a ranch on Cypress island but soon gave it up and came to Guemes to make his home. He planted an orchard of four hundred apple trees and two hundred twenty-five prune trees. Mr. O'Bryant was married twice. He had four children by the first marriage, a son, Lary, by the second marriage.

The following is contained in a letter written by Mrs. H. Humphrey Griggs of Bellingham, Washington. Mrs. Griggs is the granddaughter of John James Edens, Guemes pioneer, and she and her family maintain a summer home on Guemes in the area of the original Edens farm.

"John James Edens was born July 1, 1840, in Marshall County, Kentucky, the oldest of ten children of Thomas Edens and Lorenda Howard. Thomas Edens was an old time Whig and a close friend of Henry Clay. John Edens, as a boy, heard Henry Clay talk and learned many great lessons in patriotism and politics from him.

"The family emigrated to Illinois when John was twelve years old, then later to Knox County, Missouri, where his father settled down to farming. John attended school in both these states and at the outbreak of the Civil War he joined the Union Army and served in the 10th Missouri Cavalry. He was mustered out with an honorable discharge at Chattanooga, July 21, 1865, when he was twenty-five years old. He returned to the home farm for two years, helping his mother and younger brothers and sisters, as his father had died while he was away.

"In 1867, when he was 27 years old, he decided to strike out on his own and he headed across the plains driving an ox team to Denver, Colorado. There he remained three years working at freighting and contracting. He then went to San Francisco on the newly completed Union Pacific Railroad, went north to Portland by steamship, then over the country by stage-arriving at Olympia, Washington, at night, November 21, 1870.

In his own words he wrote about this— "Next morning after arrival I sallied forth to see the town and country. The day was foggy, dismal and rainy and my ardor was dampened, also my clothing. I returned to my hotel, disappointed and cold.

Not being acquainted with a soul on the Pacific Coast, I sought the Governor's office, introduced myself and asked for information relative to government lands subject to homestead and preemption. The Governor, E. S. Solomon, …received me kindly, told me I could not see the country to advantage during the wet winter months; that the best islands were not yet surveyed and that Whatcom County contained more good land than any other land in the territory.

I had but little money and did not propose to pay a hotel bill during the winter so went to work in a lumber camp for a while."

The following February he boarded the Steamer J. B. Libby at Seattle for the three day trip to Bellingham Bay. Arriving at the town of Whatcom, the steamer anchored off shore and Indians were out with canoes to convey passengers ashore for 25¢ each. Just seven persons came on that trip and that, the Captain said, was a large passenger list.

John Edens decided to settle on Guemes Island after rowing around and visiting the few occupants there. Humphrey O'Bryant and Jim Matthews each had a farm on the south beach. On the West beach a part of the Lummi tribe of Indians had built two longhouses for their winter's residence. So John Edens found land on the north beach of Guemes with its beautiful view of Mt. Baker and nearby islands. He preempted 160 acres, homesteaded 160 acres and located 160 acres of timberland. He built a log cabin and a saw mill and cleared the land and planted a fruit orchard. During the next few years John Edens' three brothers and a sister had taken homesteads on Guemes. Together the brothers built up a logging industry with the help of Government timber claims, natives and oxen.

There was no direct transportation to Bellingham and the closest source of supply was LaConner and they made the trip by row boat.

In a few years John Edens met Isabella Eldridge in Seholm and as she was teaching school on March Point they saw each other often. In 1880, February 24, they were married at Whatcom. They started their life on Guemes in a log cabin but as their family grew they built a larger, two story house.

Four daughters were born to them. Alice Maud (my mother), Olive Lorenda, Annette Maybelle and Mary Theresa, a baby who died at four months of age and is buried in Guemes cemetery.

When Whatcom County was partitioned in 1883, John

Edens was sent to the State Legislature as the first representative of the County of Skagit. Later, he was elected for one term to the Senate of the second Legislature as the joint representative of Skagit and San Juan counties. He was chairman of the Senate Committee on state, granted and school lands and was a member of the committee of Public Revenue and Taxation and Roads and Bridges.

In 1893, when Maud, the oldest daughter, was 12 years old, the family moved to Bellingham where the children could get a better education. They built a house on Eldridge Farm near Isabelle Edens' parents, Edward and Theresa Eldridge who had arrived there as pioneers in 1852. Henry Edens, John's younger brother, continued to maintain the home place on Guemes island for him.

After moving to Whatcom, he was appointed a member of the Board of Trustees at the Bellingham Normal (now WWSC) and served as its chairman for eighteen years, until his death.

Another one of his great interests was the "Grand Army of the Republic."

John Edens died December 24, 1914.

He sold the Guemes property in the early 1900s and my mother bought back her small piece in 1952 from Gordon and Mary Dunthorne."

And now, another pioneer, Lucius Blackinton. This man was born in Ashtabula County, Ohio, January 4, 1830. When he was nine years old his parents went to Winnebago County, Illinois, and in 1880, at the age of twenty, Lucius started across the plains in a train of eight wagons bound for California. The train wintered in Salt Lake City and, the following spring, finished their journey. Lucius worked as a young man in the California mines until 1858 with the exception of six months in Australia. In 1858 he joined the rush for the Fraser River. After a short stay he returned to California. In the spring of 1860 he came to Seattle where he worked as a lumberman. Subsequently be engaged in steam boating on the Columbia River, then worked. in a Port Orchard shipyard.

In 1872 Lucius Blackinton came to Guemes and settled on property, which, later, he sold to the Edens family. The permanent Blackinton home was on 160 acres on South Beach across from the present town of Anacortes.

Mr. Blackinton married a girl of Indian heritage and seven children were born to them. One of the daughters looked after a small store near today's Guemes ferry dock, and one son, Herman, known to his friends as "Jinxs," lives on the island above the south shore overlooking Guemes Channel. His wife died a number of years ago. An old unidentified clipping records that in May, 1890, Postmaster Blackinton of Guemes estimates the population of the island at "something over 100."

The past speaks as one walks the woods, the fields, the meadows of Guemes. That apple orchard, or part of what once was, clinging to life after so many years of growing, of blooming, and of bearing fruit—those gnarled old trees with lichen covered branches which know the flicker's bill as it bores through aged bark—those trees someone says, almost in awe, Jim Matthews planted after he came to Guemes in the mid sixties. The trees, some of them, stay on but Jim and his wife, an Indian lady, lived their years and crossed the Great Divide. Their two granddaughters, Sarah Kingston and Maud Wooten, are residents of Guemes today.

Old letters mention Jim Murrow who had a small ranch on northwest beach-Patrick (Paddy) Hyland and a son who lived on the bluff on Guemes, across from what is now Cap Sante in

Anacortes. Frequently, they rowed over the channel to sell their eggs and vegetables. Jenkins McCarthy, Id and Horace Ames and a Captain Ellis. All of these men are said to have come between 1870 and 1873. Jake Shriver, Jim Murray, Henry Hart and Kelly are remembered Guemes Islanders of that period of time.

Amanda Milfong Lee is said to have been the first white woman settler.

Timothy Mangan came to Guemes in the early seventies and built a home on the south shore facing the channel. This was a plain home and unadorned, built for shelter and practical use for a family breaking soil in a new land. After some years, according to an old photograph in a 1959 pictorial section of the Anacortes American, an attractive home, more spacious than the first, was built by the Mangans. Climbing roses shaded the front veranda, there was a shrubbery garden and, nearby, a pet deer grazed upon the grass.

Mr. Mangan also built a dock out from the shore in front of his house. It extended almost a hundred feet over the channel's waters. In years to come Alice Kellogg Cahail wrote for the Anacortes Mercury— "When the old Haroldson family came to settle on Fidalgo Island in 1876 they had to land at Mangan's landing on Guemes because there was no town of Anacortes."

Mrs. Mangan's father, Cephas Parker Woodcock, bought land on Guemes in 1876. He raised hay, the average yield as high as three and one half tons to the acre.

Mr. Woodcock was born in the state of New York in April 1815. When a small boy he moved with his parents to Ohio and from there to Missouri. He grew to manhood and became a large land owner, there, in Andrew County and served as county judge for nine years.

Mrs. Mangan, his daughter, was one of five children and the

land owned by her and her husband adjoined that of her father, Mr. Woodcock.

In 1873 there were eight or ten children on Guemes. Their parents felt there should be a school for them and a log cabin was built on the south bluff east of the landing. Mrs. Laura Murrow, daughter of Humphrey O'Bryant, mentioned as one of the island's pioneers, was the first teacher. School started in 1875.

Nathan B. Lewis played the fiddle and when his work in the field on the island was finished for the day he would come in smiling, gather children around him and play old time tunes one seldom hears today. For, along with their work, pioneers made time for pleasure. Picnics on the beach, walks through the Guemes woodland, a visit to the Indian village or, perhaps, a stay of a few days at the home of a friend to help bring the sick back to health or to care for a new mother and a little life, just born. And, sometimes, if the channel waters were calm, rowing to the "other side" was a refreshing change. There, buying a few necessities or, as a luxury, muslin for a new dress, shoes for children, boots for the man who tilled the soil—all of this was an event.

The name "Causland" will never be forgotten on Guemes Island, and the telling of the pioneering of this family will depict, in many respects, the diligence of other early settlers and their accomplishments. However, the Causland family left a special legacy, one of bravery and patriotism, which their son, Harry, bequeathed to to his Guemes Island home, when he gave his life for his country during World War I.

Alice Kellogg Cahail and her husband, Earl Cahail, were close friends of the Causland family, and Mrs. Cahail wrote the following information for the historical records of Guemes:

"Mr. and Mrs. Frank Causland left Illinois in 1885 to settle on Puget Sound. They took passage from Seattle on the steamer "Idaho" intending to explore the Nooksack Valley in Whatcom County for a home. On the boat they met Levi Erhart, who persuaded them to stop at Guemes Island to look at his homestead, which they purchased from him.

Their baggage and household goods had to be moved from the Landing on the Guemes beach through two miles of dense woods. A narrow road followed the beach as far as the William Payne place, now the Bessner farm. From there, cow paths and deer trails led through two miles of marshland, now a two hundred acre tract of fertile farm land.

With repeated trips, Frank Causland and his brother-in-law, Charley Forsay, carried a stove and other possessions to a spot already cleared in the woods. James Matthews did the heaviest hauling with a sled and a yoke of oxen.

A log house was built with an addition made of cedar shakes. The walls were papered with newspapers and a carpet covered the floor of the main room. For light they used home-made candles or carried a gallon of kerosene oil from the store at the Landing. They dug many deep wells in their search for lasting water which they never found and were obliged to settle for cisterns filled by winter rains. Water was drawn with a rope and pulley.

Some years later, a son, Harry, was born... When Harry Causland was five years old, a new house was built. Frank Causland and Jim Matthews went in a rowboat to the sawmill at Bay View where lumber for the house was purchased. They shaped it into a crude craft and towed it to Guemes with the rowboat. It was necessary to leave Bay View on the outgoing tide as the raft could not have been towed against the tide. They reached the Guemes shore at the Matthews place "without the loss of a single stick," as Frank afterwards boasted.

Then the lumber was hauled by ox team as far as the Payne place which was the end of the road. From there, they carried it on their backs on a trail through two miles of marsh and under-brush. Bricks from the Padilla Bay brickyard were also carried over the same route and a fireplace was built.

Soon after the building of the new home another son, Herbert A. Causland, was born....

At that time there were fifteen families, including bachelors, on Guemes.

Two small steamers had established a schedule and stopped at Guemes periodically. The pursers, for a slight charge, took island produce to some market, sold it, then purchased supplies for the settlers and delivered them at the Landing on Guemes. Once Mrs., Causland left a note saying she needed a nursing bottle for her baby. A purser on one of the steamers read it and on its next call at Guemes Mrs. Causland had the bottle.

"Old skid roads and huge moss covered stumps still bear wit-ness to the extensive logging operations which were carried on, on Guemes, through the years.

Mr. and Mrs. Causland always kept a beautiful lawn and luxuriant flowers. In later years they propagated an outstanding dahlia which they named "Pride of Guemes."

One spring, soon after coming to Guemes, Frank Causland and Charley Forsay secured seed potatoes from Thomas Sharpe, of Rosario, father of Wallace Sharpe. The potatoes produced so bountifully that they named them the "Tom Sharpe" potatoes. That seed was popular on Guemes for many years.

Strawberries sold to the Anacortes market provided an early summer income for the Guemes pioneers. The berries were car-ried by band to the Landing and taken across the Channel in a rowboat.

Produce from Fidalgo and Guemes Islands captured many blue ribbons at annual pioneer fairs. The Causland family always figured prominently in the list of winners.

With the outbreak of World War I, Harry Causland entered the service at Camp Kearny and was sent to New York for shipment to Europe. The following letter to Mrs. Fannie Causland from her son's bunkmate describes the act of heroism in the performance of which Harry met his death:

There follows a copy of a long letter from Harry's friend, D. A. Emerson, Co. "K" 357th Infantry American E. F. Germany-written February 28, 1919. Only a part of the letter is quoted.

"I last saw him just before we started over the top, Oct. 23, 1918. He was feeling fine and in good spirits. He had been out on patrol and had helped to capture the first German there. Next day we went over the top again on the Bantheville hill where we met with the stiffest enemy resistence of the whole drive. It was on this hill that Harry was killed.

A corporal and two men were out in front with a machine gun in a shell hole. The Germans were pressing us hard and were putting over a machine gun and artillery barrage that threatened to annihilate us as they were flanking us on both sides.

The men with the machine gun out in front ran out of ammunition and were in a helpless condition. They called back to the carriers for more ammunition but all the men refused to go across the open space because it meant certain death. Finally, Harry grabbed two boxes of ammunition and started to the machine gunners. He made it across the open space through a torrent of machine gun fire from the enemy and had just reached his objective when he fell. By getting the ammunition to the machine gunners he not only saved their lives but made it possible for them to hold back the enemy.

I did not witness any of this myself but Wardner Davie, a friend of Harry's from Bellingham, was with him at the time and witnessed the entire action. Wardner Davie is with me now and I have been talking with him about Harry. . . . You have lost a son that any mother would have been proud of. He often spoke to me of his mother in very loving terms. While your loss is great, you can indeed be proud of the service he performed in sacrificing his own life. I am proud of the fact that he was my friend."

General Pershing, writing of Harry Causland, said: "With the ammunition he carried, the gun crew stemmed the tide of counter-attack; Americans pressed forward to victory; so it was, but without his knowledge, that Private Causland, as a golden star, joined the company of one hundred heroes whose magnificent deeds General Pershing has immortalized."

The body of Harry Causland was buried in the little cemetery on Guemes Island.

Later, a park in Anacortes was given his name. The paving stones in the park of native rock, were brought from Waldron Island and the stone masonry and planting of shrubbery were done by a Mr. LePaige, a skilled artesian, secured from Europe by Gus Hansen, chairman, at the time, of the Park Board.

The park had originally been called, "Great Northern Park" since the site had been given to Anacortes by the Great Northern Railway Company. Upon request that the park name be changed, honoring Harry Causland, the Board of Directors of the railroad company headed by Louis W. Hill, wrote

"It is certainly fitting that America and American cities should recognize and perpetuate the memory of the heroic conduct displayed by our troops and individual soldiers in the World War. We appreciate not only the motive which prompted the change in the name of the park but also appreciate the feeling displayed by the city in taking the matter up with us regardless of the fact that all of the contract obligations have apparently been fulfilled and that they could make such a change without bringing the matter to our attention, and, while under the circumstances the consent of this company is not necessary. I shall be glad if you will convey to the city authorities of Anacortes our appreciation of their having brought the matter to our attention and say to them that we unreservedly endorse their action and will be glad to see local heroism recognized by the change they contemplate."

Also, today, honoring the memory of the son of Guemes Island pioneers, are the Causland American Legion Post and Auxiliary.

Henry Howard, Hal Finch, the Suttons and the Perry family —these names call to us from the pioneer, past of Guemes.

CHAPTER THREE

WHEN MARY MERCHANT was a small girl her parents often said to her "Kelly, the smuggler, will get you if you aren't good!" When she heard these words, Mary's fear was real. The name "Kelly" brought terror to the hearts of the children of Guemes Island.

There is no record of Kelly, the smuggler, ever having harmed children. But he was, for a period of about twenty-five years, a ruthless, lawless and notorious character in the region of Puget Sound. Much information concerning him, though problematical, seems to fit. Official mention of him in the United States Customs files verifies certain of his misdoings.

The story of Kelly has been related many times, publicly, through newspapers, and, also, via the grapevine from one person to another. It is not an unfamiliar chapter in the history of Guemes but must again be told because this inglorious man made the island a part of his life.

There is a place on Guemes on the south west shore called "Kelly's Point" and that is where Kelly, the smuggler, built a cabin for himself and his wife sometime between 1872 and 1878. The cabin was hidden in the woods but Kelly had only to walk to the edge of the Point to survey Rosario Strait and Bellingham and Guemes Channels.

Kelly smuggled his wares from British Columbia to various points in Washington. He smuggled wine, opium and even human beings. The latter were Chinese who were anxious to labor in America and who had entered through Canada. Kelly was paid a price by them but because of his fear of being caught while enroute by United States Customs officers he took extra precaution. When danger threatened and his boat was trying to outrun that of the law he is said to have bound his passengers and dumped them overboard to drown. When the pursuers caught up with him there was no human cargo aboard except himself and any assistant and accomplice he may have had. He also smuggled furs and other easy selling commodities-all not within the law, taken from Canada, and the opium he secured came along with the Chinese who arrived in British Columbia.

Kelly's "sloop" was well known and recognized by Guemes residents and Farmer Dirks, writer for the Bulletin in, Anacortes, gives this description of Kelly personally, quoting the words of author Stewart-Edward White - tHe looked like a tough customer. He had a round head, thick brown hair, tousled and uncombed, and a bushy beard grown high up his cheek bones, so stiff and wiry it thrust forward at a truculent angle from his chin. His eyes were small, slightly bloodshot. They stared steadily and belligerently…He was short and broad with a chest like a barrel …He wore a thin shirt and overalls-both dirty-and, apparently, nothing else. His feet were bare and so browned that evidently this was their usual state."

When someone mentioned Kelly's name to a Mrs. Lefla Claghorn, "she shivered a little as if in fear." "Oh, I remember Smuggler Kelly," she said, "He was bowlegged. He had a little dog that followed him. Whenever we saw Kelly we crossed to the other side of the street just the sound of his name, when I was a small girl, made us kids tremble with fear." This was part of one of Farmer Dirk's columns and he also quoted Mr. Palmer, owner of the first hack service in Anacortes, "Oh, I knew Kelly. Not intimately, you understand. Kelly was a bad one."

Kelly was not averse to stealing whatever he needed, tools, a cable, anything-once it was five boxes of codfish from Matheson's wharf in Anacortes, and a row boat from Matthews landing on Guemes.

Farmer Dirks learned of the sailing ability of the awesome Kelly. "Ray Robinson, Jr., took time out from duties at the fish cannery the other day to declare:

"I was a young man when Kelly was in his prime. Kelly took the "Katy-Thomas" out in all kinds of weather. Nothing was too rough for him. He didn't know what it meant to reef a sail.

One time I was over in Secret Harbor on Cypress. A hurricane was blowing. I looked across toward Anacortes. Presently I made out a ketch-rigged sloop making it across the channel like a greyhound, lower rail awash and almost keeled completely over.

Pretty soon Kelly came into the bay as unconcerned as if he had been out for a pleasant day's sail. Believe me, Kelly was a cool one and he knew his sails."

Kelly had a second hide-a-way. It was on Sinclair Island. There he had another sloop "Alert." And after Kelly had been fined many times, served terms in jail, finally in May 1909, he was sentenced to a year in McNeil Island penitentiary. When released he seemed unable to make his way in a lawful manner and, after application to the Daughters of the Confederacy, was admitted to a Confederate soldiers' home in Louisiana, where he later died.

Those who have written and spoken of Kelly seem to have no record of his wife, nor do they know whether there were children in the family. They say that Kelly's first name was Lawrence. They say, too, that he once served in the British Armed forces, went to sea afterwards and landed as a sailor in New Orleans when the Civil War was just beginning. He stayed in America and fought for the Confederacy in the Louisiana Tigers.

Also, those who looked backward to the days of Lawrence Kelly, the smuggler, have said that with all of his misdeeds, and there were many, this man always paid his debts when he had made a promise to do so.

What made Lawrence Kelly what his deeds proved him to be, what brought him to smuggling, killing and evading the law when he reputedly had served a patriotic cause for two countries England and America? What made him do all of these things during his eventful life? No one knows. Perhaps even Kelly, the smuggler, himself, never understood.

The little sloop, the "Katy-Thomas" which had carried Kelly and his illicit cargo over so many waters for so many years disappeared from the Guemes area when its master's ignominious career came to an end. No one knew where she was. Perhaps no one thought about the sturdy craft which had seemed so much a part of the life of an infamous man.

Then, unexpectedly, in 1955 the Katy-Thomas was found.

In that year the Anacortes Bulletin ran a series of articles written by Farmer Dirks.

"It was Ray Robinson, the local mariner, (Anacortes resident) who put us in touch with the Katy-Thomas Story. Stopping by, he said:

"The other day I had a curious little sailboat on my marine ways. The masts were gone. Part of the house is caved in. But if I'm not mistaken, the boat once belonged to Smuggler Kelly."

All of which whetted our interest to discover if the boat mentioned by Robinson really belonged to the first pirate of the

San Juans.

"The boat," Robinson explained, "is owned by an ex G.I. His name is Hans Wold. Hans lives with his mother aboard the old Rosalie out at the end of the Shell dock."

The Rosalie, we soon found, was a former small passenger vessel. It plied between Bainbridge and Seattle.

Now the port holes were covered over. Gently it rose and fell to the motion of water alongside the float.

On the other side of the float was a craft which hardly merited a second glance. A gull blinked a cold eye from a perch near the stem. A part of the deck had been cut open. Lines sagged to the dock.

As we stood there contemplating the old bull, Pete Peterson, well known along the waterfront, drew near. A man appeared on the deck of a black hulled tug. Peterson said "This man says this little sailer used to belong to Smuggler Kelly."

I stepped aboard the sailer. Peterson verified the fact it had been a sailer by saying the two masts had been cut off by a man who owned it before Wold.

"He cut the masts up piece by piece for firewood," he said. "She was ketch rigged. See how far astern is the second mast?"

Standing on the silent, deserted deck, I thought of all the material I had come across in the old newspaper files concerning Smuggler Kelly. People of reliable character described in almost whispered tones, how Kelly used to smuggle Chinamen down from Canada. Also opium and contraband furs.

I stepped down into the galley. There was a stove, rusted with age; cabinets where food had once been stored. On a shelf, two or three small reed mats. More than anything else the mats bore home the fact that in its youth the sturdy little ship had trafficked in Chinamen.

From the deck, Peterson called "You can find out more about her when Wold gets home. Hans is a painter over at the base. He'll get here about 5:30…"

Asked about the Katy-Thornas, Wold said he had gone to a "boneyard" in Seattle where, in the course of time he had purchased the "Rosalie" with the idea of doing over the inside and making it livable. "But even when I bought the Rosalie I noticed the squat little mastless sailer moored at an adjoining dock," Wold said. Farmer Dirks continued—

"It was at this point Wold handed over the papers on the little vessel. The papers agreed with figures on record in Robinson's office, 1930 edition of marine registry.

Katie-Thomas: sloop. Number 161054; gross 8.06 tons; net 7.66; built 1894. Waldron Is. Wash; length 38 feet 1 inch; breadth 12 feet; depth 3.6 feet. Registry, Seattle, Wn."

"Built in 1894! The boat was 61 years old! And still afloat!" Farmer Dirks marveled.

Wold said: "Old as she is, she sounded okay. She has oak ribs. On the keel is about 1500 to 2000 pounds of weight. That's what makes her ride so low in the water. … I made the fellow at the boneyard an offer. It wasn't much. He said he would have to get in touch with a lady named June Hulse. I left my address. After a time he phoned, saying that my offer had been accepted. I had her towed to Anacortes."

Almost twenty years have passed since Hans Wold bought the Katie-Thomas and since Farmer Dirks Wrote his articles concerning her in the Anacortes Bulletin—

Perhaps, somewhere, the staunch little sloop, with two new masts and flying sail, roams the restless seas as once she did with the fearless smuggler Kelly.

When a pioneer had sought and found a place on Guemes where he wished to make his home, if that place gave unspoiled wilderness, to him it was a paradise. And, if he had labored diligently and honorably with no thought of irreverence or desecration, he must have paused as he tilled his field, toiled within his woodland or took food from nearby waters, when word came to him that crime with all its brutality had found his island.

Crime, ugly and gruesome, came to Guemes.

As told by long time residents, Amos Johnson, an early settler, lived in a log cabin on the west shore. Across the country road he had some forty acres of land where he kept his farm animals. Near his cabin were a slough and a small foot bridge.

Rumor had it that Amos had money and that he had hidden it in various places on his property. Some of it, people said, was buried under the foot bridge, some under two maple trees near his cabin. Inside his one room house was a trap door, adding to the assumption he had something to hide. His bed was placed in a secluded corner where it could not be seen and he could not be harmed from the outside, through the cabin window, as he slept.

One day, a Guemes resident came by carrying mail. He heard the milch cows in Amos Johnson's pasture bawling and stamping, apparently in distress.

"Well," he told himself— "Amos will soon come along and care for them." But the next day when he came by, the animals were even more frantic.

He went to the cabin, opened the door and looked inside. Amos was not there. He went to Anacortes and reported all of this to the law and certain men went to find Amos. The cabin was still empty. After a long search, bloodhounds scented tracks to the water's edge and there were signs in flattened grass that something, no doubt the body of Amos Johnson, had been dragged from his home and taken away in a small craft which some Guemes Island resident reported having seen anchored nearby, in Bellingham Channel.

A present day resident of Guemes was told by old settlers when she was a small girl that for a short while Amos had a companion in the cabin, a man who was ill and wanted Amos to give him money for, medical care. Amos refused and the friend—if he was a friend—went away. People asked themselves "Did he kill Amos?" Or, they wondered, did unknown unscrupulous men who were aware Amos buried his wealth-did they come to force him to reveal its hiding place and in so doing injure him fatally? Or did he die of a heart attack during the struggle?

The mystery of Amos Johnson's death was never solved. Some of the gold was dug from under one of the maple trees but before more could be uncovered a road was built over its hiding place, said to be under a second one near his home.

The little log cabin, today, leans, ready to fall, a sad reminder of man's cruelty and greed.

Two men lived in the deep woods on the slope above North Bank on Guemes. They were "loners," kept to themselves, never making a friendly gesture toward anyone.

One day, one of them was found hanging from the limb of an evergreen tree-dangling at the end of a rope.

His companion said he didn't know how it happened—he hadn't done it and had no idea what person had so ended the life of his friend. "They did a lot of drinking in that cabin" was a prevalent opinion.

Maybe the victim hung himself. Who knew? No clues, no proof of murder, no anything except that a man had died.

Another unsolved island mystery.

Years later, after many pioneers had lived their lives and gone, a murder occurred on Guemes and this time the one who committed it was apprehended.

A badly beaten man was found dead on South Beach. He and a companion, neither of whom residents of the Island, quarreled over some minor matter, leading to death for the one and payment of a killer's penalty for the other.

So it was, that violence came to Guemes, a part of its history, a bitter memory, but true—

Life, though, has a way of balancing tragedy with intermittent humor.

Two eleven-year old Guemes boys, Eugene Strom and Gordon Showalter, had heard the story of Amos Johnson's death, of the Guemes hanging, too. They were deeply impressed and often visualized these sordid happenings with fear and trembling. It was all a variance from the usual occurrence in a boy's life and something to be considered. It had made them aware that untoward events could take place.

Free from school on a Saturday, Eugene and Gordon hiked along West Beach. They had reached the area where the Indian Village had once been. Here they saw a small boat, beached at the water's edge, partially covered by a piece of canvas. The boys were interested but went on with their hike as far as "the point" a mile or so away.

On their return toward home, they neared the boat again. This time Gordon's curiosity prompted him to go close, reach down and raise the canvas.

"A dead man!" he screamed and the two boys ran in terror from the scene. Gordon, unnerved and shivering from what he had seen, tottered as he ran on unsteady feet and clung to Eugene's arm for support.

At the Strom home they told Eugene's elder brother of the dead man in the boat and their quivering and cold sweat convinced the young man that this was no idle tale. He rushed to the telephone and called the coroner in Mount Vernon. This meant that the drive from there and the crossing of the channel would take a while. The brother and the two boys raced down the beach to the boat.

Raising the canvas they were confronted by the gaze of a happy man. There he lay—relaxed and smiling, holding an empty whiskey bottle affectionately in his hand.

"You're not dead!" Gordon half whispered

"Nope!" said the man. He began climbing out of the boat.

"The coroner!" the older brother rushed for home and telephone. But the coroner and his hearse had already left Mount Vernon. The two men met later on a Guemes road and the hearse went home unoccupied.

Eugene and Gordon went through a period of agony, being laughed at far and wide, but both, grown to manhood, relish the telling of the dead man in the boat.

The dead man was a troller and a drinker and all he wanted was his boat, the fish he caught and the canvas to shade him during his frequent intemperate siestas.

CHAPTER FOUR

SOME OF THE pioneer wives often worked with their husbands in the field and one of them proved beyond doubt her dedication to mode of life on Guemes island.

The husband of this lady, in appreciation, wishing to reciprocate in some special way, said to her— "As soon as I've saved enough money I'm going to buy you a diamond ring!"

Her answer has come down the road of history

"I think," she told him, "I think I'd as leave you'd buy me a cow."

And life went on among the pioneers of Guemes, out of the sixties, the seventies, the eighties and into the nineties. The span of earthly existence ended for some, others, who were left, continued to play their part in community life. Children were born and a new generation on Guemes began to grow.

Nate Lewis, after a day of logging, still played his proverbial fiddle. —Mrs. Murrow had a small organ which was carried from place to place for her, to play, as needed. "Old man Shultz" (so referred to by his friends) had his violin and this three piece orchestra, fiddle, organ and violin, made music for many a dance in the kitchen of the Mangan home and later in the small Mangan store. And when snow fell "old man Whaley's" team of oxen pulled the home made sleigh padded with straw, filled with merry pioneers. On summer days, when the sun shone, there was more leisure, it seemed, because dark ness was so long in coming.

Now there were several small steamers stopping at the Guemes landing-taking produce for sale and bringing supplies needed by the Guemes settlers. It was no longer necessary to go to the water's edge and start "hollering" across the channel asking somebody to get into a rowboat and "bring a starting of yeast." Louise Pinneo, who lived on Guemes for many a year, now in Anacortes, recalls that in the earlier days only the steamers "George E. Starr" and "Idaho" made regular stops at the southside for mail, passengers and wood. With extra steamers the early settlers felt they were given. good service.

Anacortes, which had been a scant colony of people, had begun to grow into what people called a town. There, among a number of buildings, were the Wilson Hotel in 1890-telephone service in 1897-a general store on the main floor of the Pioneer Hotel, a livery stable, and forty-seven saloons. A pioneer edition in 1959 of the Anacortes American shows a picture of the first Presbyterian Church in 1890 and says— "The sudden emergence of a city from a forest wilderness found some phases of life on Fidalgo island wanting ... it seemed unable for the time being to keep pace with spiritual needs-nonetheless, church groups were activated swiftly and although it was some years before their edifices could match the grandeur of more commercial ventures, their influence was felt from the beginning ... momentarily set back by the impact of the boom, Christian forces rallied to march into the thick of action, warring resolutely on saloons, bordellos and individuals of their moral turpitude. The beachhead, once established, churches assumed permanent position and influence in life and activity of the community."

Though horses pulled wagons through Anacortes streets

deep with mud in winter and as deep with dust in summer, for Guemes islanders the town had acquired a quality of permanence and they felt that just across the channel they had a solid neighbor.

Several clippings cut from some early Anacortes newspapers present scenes of happenings on or concerning Guemes island:

"SHIP HARBOR JUSTICE
"March 24, 1883-An election for justice of the peace of Ship Harbor precinct to fill the vacancy made by the resignation of F. A. Graham, held at Anacortes last Saturday, Chas. W. Beale was chosen without opposition. At an election held on Guemes Island for justice, out of four candidates, Mr. T. B. Mangan was elected."

"SPECULATION RIFE
"March 31, 1883-A steamer came into the harbor last week and discharged a cargo of lumber at Mangan's wharf on Guemes Island. Speculation was rife as to what this lumber would be put to, and there was a rumor afloat that the 0. R. & N. Co. would build a wharf and extensive warehouses on Guemes Island; but it turns out, according to a well-posted citizen, that this lumber excitement has no other significance than that our friend Mangan has established a lumber yard at his place."

"LOGGING ON GUEMES
"June 30, 1883-Edens' Logging camp on Guemes Island is getting out about 75,000 feet of logs per week."

"DIVISION OF WHATCOM
"Sept. 15, 1883—A petition is being circulated at LaConner and

on the Skagit to divide Whatcom county. The line of division is to be on the Chuckanut Mountains and running west between Cottonwood and Guemes island, bringing Guemes, Cypress and Fidalgo islands into the southern portion and making LaConner the county seat."

"THE TWO-CENT STAMP
"Sept. 22, 1883—October I will bring two cent stamps for letter postage."

"UNTIMELY SWIM
"Nov. 31, 1883—A yoke of oxen belonging to Wm. Whaley of Guemes Island fell from Mangan's wharf into the water Thursday of last week, dragging after them the sled to which they were hitched. The tide being out at the time, the oxen were able to wade to shore without much harm resulting from their involuntary bath in the briny deep."

"SURPRISE PARTY
"Nov. 31, 1883—A surprise party consisting of the neighbors of J. J. Edens of Guemes Island and including some friends from Fidalgo Island, visited the domicile of that gentleman on Friday evening and spent the night in dancing, plays and games. Baskets containing lunch were brought along by the visitors and served at midnight. Mr. Whaley hitched up his bay team which had recovered from the effects of their bath in the dark waters of the Guemes Channel a few days before, and brought up the laddies. The music was furnished by Prof. Lewis."

"SCHOOL HOUSE ON GUEMES
"Oct. 10, 1885—A neat and comfortable new school house, 20

by 30 feet in size, has been erected near the center of Guemes Island on the farm of William Edens, who has donated an acre of land for the purpose. The house was built by subscription, except $160 contributed from the public school fund, the ranchers donating from $1 to $20 each, in work or money. It is neatly finished, with rustic outside and ceiled within, and speaks well for the public spirit of the islanders. Another subscription is now in order for desks and seats, such as will not break the backs of the rising generation. They should get seats that a grown man would be willing to sit in six hours a day and five days a week for five years of his life."

And from a Homecoming edition of an Anacortes paper- probably the "American," which pictures life in the vicinity from 1879 to 1954—

"INDIAN INJURED

October 20, 1883—A very aged Indian was brought from Guemes Island to Anacortes Friday with a fearful wound through his hand, caused by the discharge of a gun. No one here could understand from his Chinook explanations how the accident happened. The charge passed completely through his hand, tearing and mangling the flesh in a fearful manner, but apparently not breaking any of the bones. The wound was dressed by Dr. Bowman and the Indian was tolerably comfortable at last accounts."

In the same edition is a photograph of Timothy Mangan's home taken in the mid-seventies. Beneath the picture, this description—

"Among Guemes' Pioneer Settlers was Timothy Mangan who migrated west from Missouri in the early seventies to locate

on what be described as one the 'world's most picturesque islands
in one of the world7s most picturesque settings.' Pictured is the
Mangan housestead on the southern side of the island facing
Anacortes. In the immediate forefront is the first dock which
served both boats and passengers commuting between the island
and the mainland."

Two newspapers, yellowed with age—saved by someone from
an unspecified edition of the year 1884—are noteworthy.

One tells us that on March 29th the Woodcock home on
Guemes burned, "destroying almost everything in the building.
... On account of the mildness and geniality of the climate at
this season of the year, the family will be able to live in a temporary structure till the house is rebuilt, which will be commenced
immediately."

The second clipping dated July 19—

"We learn from a reliable source that the copper mine on Guemes
will soon be reopened and operated. This mine was sunk into
the mountains some four hundred feet and numerous veins have
been found of copper assaying as high as 25 per cent of pure
copper with $5 of gold and $10 of silver to the ton. There is
also a good showing of lead and galena in some of the veins.
Immense quantities of ore are in sight and it is believed will
pay large dividends when the mine is properly developed. It is
located across the Guemes Channel, opposite and in plain view
from the Enterprise office and not an eighth of a mile from the
waterfront on the land of H. P. O'Bryant."

Apparently no worthwhile results came from the mine at
this time and, once more, it was abandoned.

There was a business transaction, too, on Guemes, when

Ephriam Funk sold a claim he had taken in 1878 to Bill Payne in 1889. And in that same year, another pioneer by the name of D. L. Marsh, arrived upon the island.

New people were finding Guemes, clearing land, building-homes, taking part in the general life of the island. Most of the residents were dedicated, hard working people. But, in their memoirs, early settlers mentioned a few among them as taking their produce across the channel, selling it and then spending the money in saloons, forgetting to come home and "letting their critters go hungry." All of this made of Guemes an average community insofar as the human side was concerned, the home of men of varied traits.

Charlie Gant came to Guemes one day in the early nineteen hundreds.

Today this man would be referred to as "an alcoholic," with an illness which, if taken in hand and treated through proper channels, could be eliminated.

In Charlie Gant's day, he was considered in plain, unvarnished words, "a drunk," the terminology of his time.

No one was more aware of his weakness than Charlie, himself. Perhaps it was this consciousness which gave him such deep compassion and understanding as he looked into the lives of his fellow man.

Charlie was a newspaper man. What he believed he wrote in words for all to read. Though his weakness was apparent in his insobriety, his fearlessness and strength shone from the ink of his pen.

Charlie admitted deserting a family in a southern Oregon town. He wrote that twelve years before coming to Guemes he had been in the Gray's Harbor area and a letter from the

Concrete, Washington, "Herald" editor says Charlie had been a friend he remembered as a child, in Anacortes.

"I think," the editor wrote, "I have a copy of the paper he put out completely in rhyme. I have also seen a book of his poems but can't remember who had it.

As I remember him, Charlie was a congenial drunk. He worked when necessary and when the spirit moved him and didn't worry much about deadlines with his paper "The Beach Comber." He had a shop down on First Street when I was a kid, later moved across the channel to an old buildings on Guemes."

During his time on Guemes, Charlie produced two small newspapers . The first he titled "The Tillikum," the second, as referred to in the previous letter, "The Beach Comber." The first edition of The Tillikum came to the people of Guemes in April, 1912, "A. L. Lewis, publisher and owner, Chas. Gant, editor and manager." In April, 1913, Charlie and Mr. Lewis were arrested and charged with having published and sent through the mails matter not allowed by the postal laws. They were released on five hundred dollar bonds. At the trial later Charlie was found guilty and Mr. Lewis was exonerated. Charlie paid a fine of two hundred fifty dollars.

Whether the court affair ended the association of the two men is not in any available record, but a few months later, in September of 1913, Charlie formed a partnership with the "Bellingham Argus" and it was rumored that the Tillikum plant was to be put on a barge and moved to Bellingham.

After the lawsuit it appears that Mr. Lewis resigned as publisher and Charlie changed his motto. This was in 1913. The new motto stated: "No Boss to Serve. No mission to perform." Shortly after that the Tillikum went out of print.

Wherever the plant went, Charlie stayed on Guemes Island.

Though the Tillikum had had a short life some of its contents should be part of its history. It was published every Tuesday— while it lasted—and Charlie stated, at "One Dollar a year, Twenty years $18.00 and two hundred years, $150, in advance." The motto of the Tillikum was— "Peel Bark While the Sap's up."

In the editorial column of the first issue of the Tillikum, "Don't be a dampfool and yell failure because the Tillikum is small. You wasn't very large yourself when you were first born."

One column Charlie labeled— "Clam Nectar-Stimulating paragraphs from the pen of the Tillikum's Cheerful Idiot."

Items:

"The first prohibition law ever passed was written by an old man by the name of Moses 4000 years ago and became in full force and effect on and after its first publication. There were ten sections of it and every section has been violated by some of the human race every day since that legislator of the wilderness episode carved its provisions on tablets of stone. Show me a living human being between the age of 6 and 90 years, possessed of sound mind who claims to have kept the ten commandments and I will show you a most gigantic liar. The ten commandments were the first prohibition laws sprung on the people."

An election was soon to be held and Charlie wrote—

"That and candidate for legislative honors up at Mt. Vernon is said to have made the statement that he will cast the ladies' vote, that they dare not go against him, that he is next. If he made such a statement we hope the good women of Mt. Vernon will give him a goose egg, a whole settin' of 'em."

"Don't vote politics, vote for the man. The old party lines are broken and all hell can never fill the gap."

"The time is here in Skagit County politics when the members of the central committee will not be men who merely hand their proxies to the boss and remain at home. They will be men who attend meetings and exercise the right of a free man, not the duties of a political peon."

"It makes no difference which way the fight goes, democratic, republican, bull moose or dry, the Tillikum will be printed on Guemes Island. We do not depend on politics for anything except amusement and we've quit drinking-so there!"

Charlie was aware of what was happening far, from Guemes Island.

"The Turks and Greeks are mixing up in another holy war. How about that book where it reads, "Nations shall war against nation no more, the sword shall be beaten into the plowshare and the sabre to the pruning hook?" "Peace on earth, to man good will.

Paragraphs from another Tillikum column which Charlie named "Tanbark":

"We want to assist in the advancement of the interests of every man, woman and child on Guemes Island, regardless of age, sex, color or previous conditions of servitude. We may dispute the ways of some men and some women, but regardless of our personal likes or dislikes we are for the whole of Guemes Island."

"We realize as well as you do-some of you-that you are not loving the Tillikum to death, but the most of you who don't like it are borrowing it every week. We have a list of Anacortes Tillikum borrowers a mile long. You son-of-a-gun, you are one of them."

"We believe the majority of the Guemes school board favor the putting in of more windows in the primary department. No one man is the boss of the Guemes School District."

Charlie Gant resented any criticism of Guemes Island. For the land and most of its people he had eternal praise and encouragement. So when someone spoke against either or both, he retaliated unreservedly. In the Tillikum of September 17, 1912:

"THE DIRTY DOZEN

Some low down dirty knocker over on the Anacortes side is circulating the information that Guemes Island land will raise nothing. We know who the dirty duck is and if he don't stop it we shall tell our good people all about that widow that he robbed and the mortgaged property be sold back yonder. Guemes land is the same as Fidalgo island land, it will raise anything that is planted and cultivated and lots of it. We invite all the strangers who visit Anacortes, to come to Guemes and see the crops of wheat, oats, hay, potatoes, onions, cabbage," carrots, parsnips, beets, peas, beans and every other kind of vegetable we can raise, along with our health giving ozone . . ."

"J. SHRIVER'S FINE FRUIT

John Shriver, one of the highly esteemed old timers of Guemes Island, is another of our well to do farmers who comes forward and refutes the statement that Guemes soil will not produce remunerative crops. Mr. Shriver has been farming on this fertile island for many years and each succeeding year proves conclusively that the very best of fruits, berries, vegetables and cereals can be produced here. Mr. Shriver delivered at the Tillikum office, Tuesday morning, some of the finest apples and blackberries we have ever had the pleasure of seeing in this state or any other and the editor of this great weekly has stolen apples from every state in the Union where they grow and they are grown in 48 states."

"JACK KIDD'S ONION CROP

When a man can raise 22 sacks of the finest onions in the whole world on a strip of ground twenty-four feet wide and 85 feet long, there is not much show for the knocker who is circulating the report that things will not grow on Guemes Island. Jack Kidd, one of the best known men on the island has just harvested the above named crop and averaging one acre, would produce 23 tons of onions. At the average market price the one acre of ground would produce $720 worth of onions.

Mr. Kidd produced single onions that weighed better than a pound each and has in his garden many carrots and beets which are far too large for the market. Mr. Kidd also raised canteloupes, tomatoes, beans and cucumbers all of good quality and prodigal in quantity."

A paragraph from Tanbark column in the same edition—

"Some data hunter over at North Yakima writes us and wants to know who the first man was that paid the death penalty by hanging. It was Judas Iscariot, brother, a pious pretender who betrayed Jesus of Nazareth with a kiss in the Garden of Gethsemane. He tried, convicted and executed himself with a scarlet cord taken from a harlot named "Myriam," on the Barbara Coast in Jerusalem."

And—

"We believe in lifting the fallen. We believe if a girl has gone astray that she should be pittied, not persecuted. We believe that a man who has fallen into the mire of iniquity should be picked up, not trampled upon. We do not believe in crushing the fallen into the dust of the earth and rocking the holy hypocrite in the lap of luxury. We believe in humanity as God made it."

"Our object is to make a publication and to publish it on Guemes Island. Let every friend of ours, every man and woman whose sentiments we voice, get us one now cash subscriber and we will, in a short time give you a weekly magazine that will drown all trouble."

"If you want a still larger paper on Guemes, come in and subscribe for an extra paper to be sent away to a friend. We are now in need of a bigger press and that is all that stands between us and a bigger paper. Come on, boys."

The Guemes Tillikum, despite Charlie's dreams, became a part of the past. But he was a newspaper man -writing came naturally to him. His-nature demanded that he do it. So Charlie began printing another paper on Guemes-its name "The Guemes Beachcomber."

CHAPTER FIVE

HAL FINCH, an old timer from Anacortes, used to visit on Guemes and he remembered Charlie Gant. He looked backward after many years had passed-and wrote with trembling hand:

"Chas. Gant lived in a cabin near Blackintons. He seldom if ever was seen sober when he visited Anacortes. He had done editorial jobs for Anacortes newspapers but could not stay sober to hold a job. Eventually he edited and published a little gem called "The Guemes Island Beachcomber." . . . I would give 5 bucks for a copy today...Gant was a wit and a real character when and if you could find him sober."

The historical material accumulated by Gertie Howard and Meta Whicker contains twelve copies of Charlie Gant's "Guemes Beachcomber." They date from May, 13, 1916 through May 29, 1923, intermittent copies which have been found here and there by various families. A few of them have, written upon them, in pencil, the names of the old timers who owned them-Joe Skinner, R. W. McKinstry, Fred G. Abby, Mr. and Mrs. William Everett, Sr. and Mrs. Hugo Erbolm. Some of these people lived in Anacortes, but all of them read the Beachcomber.

The little paper was printed on a sheet of paper about fourteen inches high and twenty-two inches long, folded, magazine fashion so as to create four printable pages. Charlie called the paper "Independent-Published every Thursday in the Interest of the Heartbeats of Humanity." The subscription price was one dollar per annum.

The countless words which Charlie Gant wrote for the Beachcomber are, today, a priceless gift to those who value the significance of the colorful history of by-gone years on Guemes Island. This man of weakness and of strength, painted, on paper, all facets of life as he saw them on the bit of land which to him, for a period of his lifetime, was home.

How much scholastic education Charlie Gant had experienced is not known. Regardless, he had a fund of knowledge not only from the areas he had seen in his own country but of world history, literature, foreign nations. His thinking reached into antiquity. He knew the Bible and quoted from it frequently in his writings. He told the world that he did not always follow its precepts. But he seemed always to have sympathy, to be critical when he felt he saw the need, but to praise when it was, due. Charlie appeared through his newspaper pages to be a courageous man. Station did not deter him from exposing an ill deed. He did not consider personal wealth a criterion for overlooking faults. No matter what place one held in the community or in the country at large, Charlie looked inside to find the real prerequisites of a man—or of a woman.

It is unfortunate, and often the way of our world, that a man is remembered for his impropriety rather than for his integrity and well-doing. What Charlie wrote for the Beachcomber, whether be realized it or not, told what sort of a person he was, inherently. He saw the happiness and the suffering of others. He saw endeavor and accomplishment among his neighbors, his friends and the whole citizenry around and about him. He saw failure, too. He saw it in himself. He was patriotic and revered patriotism in other.

With all of these admirable characteristics, Charlie had his frailties. It is regrettable that he could not conquer his craving for drink. But, as one turns the faded little pages of the Guemes Beachcomber, the realization comes that Charlie, always seeing the beauty of nature in spring, summer, fall and winter, left a valuable legacy and one of virtue rather than depravity.

From his poem "Puget Sound, a Paradise"

> "I thank you God, for flowers and trees
>   And mountain chains and sapphire seas;
>   For winding trails and mountain slope
>   And all the pleasures born of hope.
>   I want no other land of bliss,
>   Just keep your heaven—give me this
>   This scenic Eden—Puget Sound,
>   Here's where I ever would abide
>   No fame, no gold, but satisfied."

So much of what Charlie wrote bespoke his love of the land and that, as he walked, his eyes beheld the sublimity of his world.

> "Washington, when I shall cease
>   To walk your vales and climb your hills,
>   Just let me rest somewhere in peace
>   Beside your singing mountain rills
>   Or by your sea of Heaven's blue
>   Or in your loving forest shade.
>   But just as long as it is you,
>   I don't care where my bed is made."

Most of Charlie's poems were long and only certain verses of each will be included. However, the following is given in its entirety.

GUEMES ISLAND
By Charlie L. Gant

When the sapphire waters ripple
On a stretch of agate beach,
And the rugged mountains tipple
Phantom shadows, each to each;
There's a bonnie island studded
With rare blooming orchard trees
And with forest deeply wooded
Where it borders on the seas.

Near, across the smiling waters
Spreads a wealthy land—a pride—
Where the thrifty sons and daughters
Of old Father Adam, bide
And the fruit perfume comes sweetly,
Like a fair Calypso's smile
And a solace reigns completely
Over all on Guemes isle.

Over there a city glowing
Sends its light across the seas,
Over here an orchard, blowing
Sheds its fragrance on the breeze.
And the lowing herds all grazing
Seem content in clover guile,
And the singing birds seem praising,
Every tree on Guemes isle.

All around the hills are standing
Diademed with green and snow,
Like some warriors bold commanding
All the world which lays below,
While the busy housewife singing
In a sweet and happy style
Keeps the joyous fountain springing
Love and life on Guemes isle.

'Tis the isle of sweet contentment
Where the soul of man is free,
Where we live with no resentment
Just where one would ever be.
Mere envy's tooth of rancor
Ever leaves its mark on file,
And we gladly drop the anchor
On the shores of Guemes Isle.

                                        (April, 1912)

Sometimes Charlie turned facetious in his papers, mainly the Beachcomber—

"A girl from Burlington, she built
 A fire with gasoline,
 She scratched a match upon the sill
 And hasn't yet Benzine."

And—

"A woman name of Mary
 Note She had a little boy,

And on the kid she used to dote,
He was her only joy.
Says she "He'll be a joy to me,
When large enough to vote."
The only name he ever had was Promissory Note."

Sometimes his short verse gave good advice—

"Watch your step, my little brother,
Use your noodle, little man,
Do not drop your sweetheart's letter
In the city garbage can.
Do not run your boat of true love,
On the shoals for folks to scan,
When you write to her you do love,
Do not use the garbage can."

Charlie wrote this before mini-skirts had ever been mentioned!

"There was a young girl from LaConner,
The limit she was, on my honor;
She sheared off her tresses
And shortened her dresses
Till scarcely a thing was left on her."

One of Charlie's Beachcomber columns was labeled "Sweet Peas." It was a personal column and told of the goings and comings of Guemes Islanders and their visitors from other areas.

"Many Guemes Island ladies visited the city of Anacortes Tuesday, taking well filled baskets of crochet, aprons, doilies and some other white muslin stuff on which to sew; some lace and quite a sprinkling of good things to eat.

Wm. E. Everett and wife, Billy and Margaret, visited with Grandmother and Grandfather Loring Saturday night and Sunday. Teane was absent this time. Don't let it happen again.

John Kidd was in Anacortes Tuesday attending lodge, visiting and attending to business affairs.

Mr. and Mrs. A. J. Mitchell and family of Anacortes and a Mr. Larson, enjoyed a drive about Guemes Island Sunday.

Local enthusiasts are preparing to petition Congress to change the name of Guemes to Hallelujah Island.

Frank Causland was doing some trading and attending to business matters in the city of Anacortes, Saturday.

Grandma Wooten was doing some trading in town Monday afternoon.

Grandma Mary Blackinton who has been suffering from asthma, is still kept close to her home but is some better."

Some Guemes people who knew Charlie felt that he carried within himself a deep heartache. He once wrote, and gave no explanation for writing it—

"The Vacant Chair"
  "Somehow the sun don't seem to shine
  As brightly as it did when he
  Was here, that precious boy of mine,
  That child who was the world to me.
  The birds don't sing so sweetly now
  The flowers are not so fragrant quite
  And things don't seem the same, somehow
  Since little Buster said "Goodnight."

O, birds bow once you sang when he

So gladly heard your love-note lay;
And through the woodland, menily,
He wandered with you day by day.
O flowers, how your petals blushed
 To meet his eyes of love-lit light
But flowers have withered, birds have hushed
Since little Buster said, "Goodnight."

Charlie wrote "Rest Well' dedicated to the memory of Harry Causland—World War I hero. It was published in the Beachcomber. Here is a part of it—

"Rest well, and may the smiles of God
 Shine through his sunlight gleaming,
And with a halo bless the sod
Where you, brave heart, lie dreaming.
Let star beams fall and kind winds sough,
While moonbeams, mild and tender,
Keep vigil, sentinel, for you,
Oh, mankind's brave defender.
Your brave heart did not quake or faint,
When all the world was crying
You proved yourself a martyred saint
By daring, doing, dying....
Rest beneath your cross of worth,
And we shall tell the story;
You proved yourself the salt of earth
And won immortal glory.
Sing low your lullaby, oh seas,
And birds make soft your singing,
And winds, blow lightly through the trees,

While harps keep softly ringing.
Beat low the drum, sound low the fife,
Here rests a martyred brother
Who volunteered to give his life,
And died, to save another."

This is Charlie's last poem:

"The worst regret that I shall ever know
Will be the time when I am called to go
Away from this charmed, enchanted land
Of forests green and gleaming golden sand.
I do not fear to walk the misty way
But I'll regret the going, that last day
When I shall see these dear loved isles of green
And these blue seas with breezes so serene.

I do not hope to find a fairer place
With greener isles or bluer water grace
A land so grand or life more free
Somehow, this land is always sweet to me.
Let the martyr hope—to hope he hath a right
But when I come to bid this land good-night
I shall regret that I must say the word
To isles and peaks, to seas, to bee and bird.

There may be some fair Eden, just beyond,
Of which I may, in future, be as fond
As I am now of this fair land of bliss
Where nature's lips invite a nature's kiss,
But be it known , when death and I have met

I'll bow to him, and yet, my one regret
Will be to leave these isles and seas and sand
For I believe there is no fairer land."

Charlie Gant painted a picture of himself as most men do as they live away their years. Charlie painted much of his life in the written word, prose and poetry, the poetry in the technique of his era. The painting has varied themes. It also has merit, humanity and wisdom.

Jinx Blackinton and Herb Woodfield who live on Guemes today and who knew Charlie say that he died not too far from Guemes, in Bellingham, Washington.

CHAPTER SIX

AN OLD LEDGER, forgotten for years on an unused shelf, came, once more, into the light of day. The pages of the ledger are yellow with age, the scent of mildew upon them. The cover of the book has known the feel of hands which touched the soil and left their finger imprint upon it. Someone, man or woman, wrote within the pages of the ledger what he or she had learned, not in school, but through observation upon a Guemes island farm. It must have been such a place where an early settler had a flock of chickens and was determined to know about them. He was unschooled but diligent.

Written in pencil, laboriously and specifically—

"Bird Selection.

The yellow color disappears slowly when the hen is lay form.

    1. Vent in a few days.

    2. Eye ring in about a week.

    3. Beak from root to point in four to six weeks.

    4. Legs in four to six months.

Out of the lay the yellow color will come back in the same order but from three to five times faster, this will help you to find if the hen is in lay or not. About how long a time she has been a laying or how long she has been out of lay (going into lay the comb and wattles will grow big and turn more red out "of lay they will shrink.)

The pelvic bones in a good layer are straight and not crooked. It is good if the distance between the pelvic bones is large it indicates that the hen has a roomy body to consume food and to produce a large quantity of eggs.

if the distance is only 1-1/4 inches sell her.

if 1-1/2 inches she may lay 150 first year.

if 2 inches she may lay 200 first year.

if 2-3/8 inches she may lay 250 first year.

if 2-3/4 inches she may lay 280 first year

This method can be used at any time when pullets four to five months old or reaches full maturity.

The following four things will tell you if a hen is a good layer or not:

1 capacity-the distance between the end of the breast bone and pelvic bones.

2 condition-measure by feeling if the breast bone is full or thin.

3 type—meaning if she is a layer type or beef type and can be measured by thickness of pelvic bones.

4 vitality—vigor and health.

1, 2 and 3 can only be measured by taken the hen in your hand. By feeling with thumb and forefinger how much of the breastbone is without flesh. Feel about one inch behind the front of the breastbone. Divide the first joint of your forefinger in three parts and if you can take enough of the bone between the two fingers to reach the first mark we call the hen one finger out of condition if you can take enough between your finger to reach the joint she is three fingers out of condition.

Feel thickness of left pelvic bone the bone with flesh

fat or thin.

1/16 of inch good 2/16 also good 3/16 not so good 8/16 not good for a layer 1 inch no good beef type."

In 1912 the Anacortes American stated that Guemes island was a paradise for poultry. "All breeds of chickens, ducks, geese and all members of the feathered throng of the barnyard flourish. There are no diseases or insects of dangerous nature and miles of beach lined with decayed clam shells and gravel and the island climate is admirably adapted to poultry culture and a. ready market is ever near at hand for the products of the poultry yard."

The one who studied so thoroughly the capabilities of his laying hens, according to the Anacortes American, must have had no trouble selling the eggs they put into the nests he made for them, and if, as he wrote in the old ledger, a hen would lay from 150 to 280 eggs a year, the poultry business proceeds no doubt brought to him the conviction that his research as to the life style of his cackling friends had been worth while.

Advertised for sale in 1913-a 56 acre ranch on Guemes, 25 acres under cultivation, team, wagon, buggy, harness, farming implements, 6 milch cows, 2 calves, pigs, cream separator, new 7 room house, barn 30x50, young orchard, small fruit, 500 cords of shingle bolts, 238 cords cut (purchaser to pay for the cutting) waterfront property—price $5000.00.

Guemes had its problems, those which appear as a community develops. And with the increased population of about one hundred and fifty inhabitants it was necessary to have a center of control and advice as well as for social gatherings for the enjoyment of the islanders.

In December, 1912, the Guemes Island Improvement Club was formed for "the general upbuilding and promoting of the best interests of the island, and every man has declared his intention to pull in the harness of progress." The president was W. D. Dolph, vice president, H. C. Carver, secretary, Charlie L. Gant and treasurer, Jack Kidd. Committees were formed for Publicity, Bridges, Roads and Schools, Entertainment, Transportation, Sites and Buildings, Membership and Invitation. The club met weekly.

It was necessary to have a meeting place where the club and members of the community could carry on business matters and social activities. A hall was built by Guemes men contributing their labor, and when it was finished in 1914 the whole cost was less than five hundred dollars. This was cause for celebration and a social was held to honor those who had worked hard to complete the building. Musicians were brought across the channel from Anacortes to play for the dancing.

The land upon which the hall was built not too far up the road from the ferry landing, was a gift from Jack Kidd.

As in so many newly settled areas there was a Grange on Guemes, and after the Community Hall was finished the Grange members were allowed to use the hall for six months by paying half the running expenses. If a dance followed a Grange meeting those attending from across the channel paid fifty cents a couple. Members of the Grange were not charged for dancing but had to pay fifteen cents for their supper.

The hall became the center of social life on Guemes. Today, its size increased, it is still the setting for monthly meeting of the Guemes Community Club-the aftermath of the Improvement Club organized in 1912. It is also used for rummage sales, amateur theatricals, private parties and is the scene of the famous barbecues of Guemes.

While all the progress of community activity was taking place everyone continued to be amazed at the many pounds of onions Jack Kidd could raise on a plot of ground 45x106 feet—and potatoes grown by Frank Causland on his Pleasant View Farm on Guemes. One potato weighed three pounds and others were almost as large.

The editor of the Anacortes American write "Nowhere in the world can wild roses be found in such beauty, fragrance and profusion as on Guemes Island. Guemes could make a distinct hit by giving a wild rose festival."

About the same time Guemes residents complained about Anacortes picnickers who came over, trespassed on their property, stole berries and fruit and damaged gardens and orchards.

Charlie Gant got his name in the Anacortes American by going fishing in the Bering Sea on the "Joseph Russ" and soon thereafter a ladies' group on Guemes made and presented Charlie with a flag for his newspaper office.

Charlie's enthusiasm came to the fore for Guemes again when he maintained— "There is not a spot beneath the canopy of heaven that can excel the farm of John Shriver on Guemes island."

Nate Lewis continued to log on Guemes and one who logged with him, Mark Johannson, still looks backward to those days when life on Guemes was young.

Telephone service had been established between Guemes and Anacortes in 1908 and there were thirty two subscribers. Then a tugboat came along and damaged the cable beyond repair. The Guemes telephone service was home owned, the necessary funds having been contributed by islanders themselves, but they did not have enough money to maintain the lines. The community wanted West Coast Company to purchase the system but more subscribers to telephones were needed to make this move worth while for the company.

After the first cable was broken there was a period when Guemes was again without telephone connection. Through coming years each time service was renewed by cable it was soon severed, once by a destroyer, later by a freighter of the Lucken-back Line, four times by certain boats and once by a raft of logs. These were difficult and expensive years for Guemes islanders. Finally, microwave took the place of cable. Today, telephones on Guemes are a part of General Telephone Company of the Northwest, Inc. All of this the result of those Guemes men who formed their own small company, financed and kept it for years under difficulty and finally, through their efforts, brought it to the place where a solid financial structure was willing to make it a part of its organization.

The years of World War One changed, for its duration, the course of life in the United States and Guemes was a part of it all. Young island men volunteered for military service-went away, and, as Harry Causland gave his life for the Stars and Stripes, so did the son of Sarah and George Kingston. A friend of the Kingston family, Harold Wave Whicker of Guemes wrote of this boy of Indian ancestry— "Dutch was a good six feet. He had the slender grace of a young Douglas fir." And of his relationship with his father— "They were more than father and son, these two; they were companions inseparable in the forest, on the trail, in the hunt, or upon the waters after the halibut and salmon. That was their life. They asked no more from their racial gods. . . . They were never in a hurry. They were never aloof from others. The urge for laughter and kidding would fetch them over to where I stood alone in relative amateurism. We perched upon some log. We talked men's talk of the forest and the sea. It was tall talk. This done, they helped me fall my trees."

One might hope that this boy "Dutch (Clayton), the son of

George and Sarah Kingston, far from his island home in war, during some brief interlude between sleeping and waking, relived his years on Guemes with his parents and his friend "Whick." Perhaps, for that fleeting moment his poignant memories made Armageddon seem only a dream.

In 1917 America needed ships. Before her entrance into the war Germany had sunk many trans Atlantic vessels sailing under the flag of our country and shipbuilders were working as fast as possible to replace them, especially freighters needed to carry war supplies to Europe.

Sloan Brothers of Olympia decided to build a shipyard on the south shore of Guemes near the landing, and, according to the Anacortes American and Charlie Gant's Beachcomber, five ways were completed and keels laid on each, "A steam crane on tracks was employed and five boilers installed."

Cord wood for the boilers and the plant generator came from trees logged and cut from the Guemes forests. Guemes men constructed what they termed "skid" roads for hauling wood to the shipyard.

When the community was informed that the shipyard was to be built, Guemes men joined with Anacortes business men and, together, they solicited funds and themselves donated what they could afford to build a "scow ferry' to aid in transportation during ship building days. However, six hundred men were employed and many from across the channel slept on Guemes in tents or some other temporary structure as available transportation was inadequate.

The ships were launched in 1919.

The war ended and the shipyard closed, all buildings were dismantled and the quieter routine of life on Guemes Island, returned.

And, getting back on an even keel after all the strain of war, Charlie started a new column in his Beachcomber. "Angel Talk" he called it, "By the Cheerful Idiot."

"You can't run your salvation flivver into Heaven on "oxelene," along the unpaved road of fanaticism. You've got to have the base of honesty, the smooth surface of brotherly love, the filtered gas of charity' the lubricator of human kindness in order to run the old machine through the pearly door of the jaspar wall of the golden garage of eternity. He that fails to go thus equipped will have the angels looking all over hell for him at the first harp tournament."

"The Ladies of Guemes met Feb. 21st, 1912, with Mrs. C. A. Dunn, to organize a club and elect officers for same.

This information comes from an old minute book which records the club activities through February 21, 1916. Gertrude Magill acted as secretary for a number of years.

The club members made quilts and raffled them off usually receiving no more than five dollars apiece, this, however, being commensurate with the prices of that era. Neckties were made by the ladies and sold at their meetings in the evenings when men were invited to a 94 necktie party." Once, at such a gathering the club felt elated when Guemes men purchased ties in the amount of $22.50.

Many of the old fashioned homey events were offered to residents by these Guemes women. Hard time dances, ice cream and strawberry and basket socials. At one time the club "helped Mrs. Loppe get her house in better shape" the men coming to do the work and the ladies providing a dinner. There was a stork shower for Mrs. Stone and the club mailed the gifts so she would receive them on Valentine's Day. And on a January seventeenth William Payne and John Shriver had birthdays and were honored at a social with birthday cakes. Each person paid as much admission as the years of his life. Later it was recorded that John Shriver sent his thanks for his birthday cake.

There were Halloween socials and one Christmas the club provided a tree for the Guemes school for the children and gave them nuts and candy. Later, they paid Laura Smith ninety cents for cleaning the schoolhouse after the Christmas entertainment.

This group of women did their share in the organization of an athletic club, and, on December 14, 1914, the Grange, the Guemes Island Improvement Club and the Athletic Club decided to work together and each pay what it could on the community hall debt.

The club wanted a piano. It owned a half acre of land somewhere and someone suggested it be offered as "part payment' on the price of the piano.

There were intermittent dilemmas in the group, those common to every affiliation. Sometimes a member felt maligned, and resigned. Rarely, because of some misdemeanor, someone was asked to demit. Regardless of difficulties from time to time, the good the island community received from the Women's Social Club of the early nineteen hundreds has endured and today another gathering, the Women's Club of Guemes, as did those of another day, carries on-contributing financially and socially in various ways which conform to present living among island residents.

With organization of various groups, life on Guemes was becoming channeled. It had not been so with the earliest pioneers. They were the breakers of the island soil. They were the ploughmen, the planters, the harvesters. Their lives were grooved in the land from which, through their own labor, came the food which sustained them and the farm animals which belonged to them. And, at rare intervals, when leisure came, they shared a plentiful table with neighbors who lived here and there beyond the unclaimed forest, and called it good.

CHAPTER SEVEN

HERE, ON THIS grassy slope, on central Guemes, is Edens Cemetery. This is a place of the dead. But there are those who, within their graves, live on, in history.

One cannot walk, ever so gently, over the soil of this small area, without hearing the voice of the past. It calls in silence. "Do not forget," it says, "our years on Guemes, the land we cultivated, the homes we built, the little island world we helped to make." The voice of the Guemes pioneers! For almost all of these early settlers found their last abode upon this grassy hill.

The pioneer graves are many, their names one with Guemes. There are graves of more recent and of present day residents and graves of those who died in war. Too, in this cemetery, are a few unmarked graves, eloquent because no living person can say to whom they were given.

Years ago, a resident of Guemes wrote a letter to a friend. He told of his veneration for the historic Edens cemetery and he included a quotation—the words of Oliver Wendell Holmes:

"Here, in the corner of my heart, a little plant called reverence that needs watering."

The hearts of Guemes islanders, down through the generations, turn toward the sacred hill, the grassy slope, on central Guemes.

William Edens, pioneer, owned a portion of the land which is now Edens cemetery. He had a son. He called him Willie. When Willie died his father carried him to a place "near the big rock" and buried him there. Afterward, William Edens gave his land for a cemetery. William Payne, another early settler, donated five adjoining acres which he had formerly purchased from Henry Howard. William Payne died shortly thereafter.

For many years, a day was set aside to put the cemetery in proper order for "Decoration" Day. In 1904, a cemetery deed was executed by Mary Edens with the provision that "sole use of the property is for interment of the human dead residents of Guemes Island." An archway of wood was built at the cemetery entrance.

Thirty years later the Guemes Improvement Club decided to replace the old archway with brick and cement pillars, each pillar to have an indenture for a brass plate. Mrs. Mollie Edens Finley of Bellingham, daughter of William Edens, made plans to provide a brass inscription plate on the right pillar, as a memorial to her mother who is buried in the cemetery. It was the hope that when sufficient funds were available another brass plate with the names of pioneers whose graves were also there, on the hillside, would be placed in the indenture on the left pillar.

In 1934, a dedication ceremony took place at the cemetery. The ensuing article, copied from the Anacortes American dated July 5th, tells the story

"Under sunny skies, with a background of forest trees and in the presence of many relatives and friends, Edens Cemetery on Guemes Island was dedicated to the Pioneers of Guemes. The program given was an impressive one and was as follows:

Reveille was sounded by Adjutant Charles Bennett of the Salvation Army, followed by, an invocation by Rev. R. K. Anderson of the Pilgrim Congregational Church.

Unveiling of the brass inscription plate, given by Mrs. Mollie

Edens Finley of Bellingham, was performed by Miss Eileen Finley, and Mrs. Mary Finley Healey, a granddaughter of Mr. Edens, placed a floral wreath under the plate.

The unveiling of the brass inscription in the other gate was made by the little daughter of Hubert Causland and Hubert Causland, Jr., recited "Out Where the West begins" in a very creditable manner.

Rev. Anderson gave an inspiring address and dedicated the cemetery to the pioneers of Guemes. He told of the work done by the pioneers in making Guemes ready for the descendants, and paid tribute to Harry Causland, World War veteran hero whose body rests in the cemetery there.

Music was furnished by Mrs. R. K. Anderson and her daughter, Miss Gwendolyn, Rev. Anderson and Mrs. C. L. Dwelley, with Adjutant Bennett playing the accompaniments for the hymns on his comet. A number of Guemes children and young people also aided in the singing.

Taps were sounded by Adjutant Bennett following the benediction.

The ferry had to make two trips to carry the cars across to the dedication.

The veil used for the Edens plate was loaned for the occasion by Mrs. Thomas Nicholson of Anacortes, it belonged to her mother, Mrs. Eliza Hodson.

The pioneer memorial plate was unveiled by Viola Mary Causland. A large black wool Cashmere shawl, which belonged to Mrs. Amelia Forsey, mother of Mrs. Fannie Causland, grandmother of H. A. Causland and great grandmother of Viola and Herbert Causland, Jr., was used for this plate.

Mrs. Forsey and Mrs. Causland are both resting in this cemetery.

The two large memorial wreaths were of pink snapdragons, blue scabosia and beautiful white Regal lilies. The Regal lilies were given for the occasion by Mrs. W. R. Burke, of Anacortes, and the wreaths made up by Mrs. Hubert A. Causland.

Pioneers resting in Edens cemetery are:

Mr. and Mrs. William B. Edens, Mr. and Mrs. John W. Shriver, Mr. and Mrs. Lucien Blackinton, Mr. and Mrs. James Matthews, Sr., Mr. and Mrs. James Matthews, Jr., Mrs. Jaynes A. Murrow, Mrs. Amands Wflfong Lee, Mrs. Amelia Forsey, Mrs. William 0. Krider, Mrs. Frank Causland, Mr. William Payne, Mr. Solomon Shriver, Mr. Nathan B. Lewis, Mr. James T. Sutton and Mr. Henry C. Howard."

Regardless of their human imperfections which are a part of the life span of every man, the early settlers bequeathed a worthy heritage. They had strength. They had stability, courage and purpose. They had vision. And it is the hope today, of those who covet their island, that these sterling qualities of the pioneers will be perpetuated year after year, upon Guemes.

There is a cross on the cemetery hill on Guemes. There is no grave beneath it. Someone who knew he would want it there, erected the cross in memory of R. M. Hammarlund, DSC, a boy who died on Guadalcanal, January 14, 1943, World War II. His body lies in Punchbowl, the National Memorial Cemetery of the Pacific, Honolulu, Hawaii.

Herbert Causland, Jr., looks backward and remembers when, those years ago, at the dedication of the Guemes Island cemetery, he was eleven. He remembers that he recited "Out Where the West begins" and everyone said he had done so "in a very creditable manner.

CHAPTER EIGHT

The early settlers of Guemes grew old. They grew tired. Their fingers gnarled and stiffened from clutching the axe, the hoe, the homemade plow, wanted rest. The venturesome hardihood of youth had gone from these men and women but, as they experienced the declining years of life, they could see upon the island their contribution, their lasting gift to future generations.

These pioneers had brought Guemes to the place. where its people could begin to come together as a community. Roads, rough and unfinished though they were, made it easier for families to meet for social and business affairs. The Improvement and Athletic clubs, the Women's group, the Grange, flourished. Younger residents were furthering the way for which the pioneers had broken the sod.

There was no church on Guemes. If a pioneer prayed, it must have been within the sanctity of his home or, perhaps, as he tilled his land, he looked upward and thanked God for what he had come to call his own, on Guemes.

But now a group of people on the island wanted to build a church, a place of worship. They had, during the Spring and Summer of 1914, with the Reverend J. D. Hudson, Congregational minister from Pilgrim Church, of Anacortes, been conducting religious services "in a hall controlled by a Ladies Club and situated on the main road across the Island, from North to

South and about one half mile from the beach at the South end of the road." The foregoing quote was taken from an old minute book and said to be part of an "Historical statement regarding the organization of the Guemes Congregational Church located on Guemes Island, Skagit County, State of Washington."

Services which had been held in "a hall," continued in the school house, further along on the main road on the island. There, on September 17, 1914, the Guemes Congregational Church was organized. Ten adults and two children became charter members, their names Frank and Gertrude Magill, Leora Goodwin, Lumena Spencer, Ellen Griffiths, Ola A. Goodwin, Fay Young, Harlow Magill, Laurence Smith, Ida Smith, Ervin Spencer, Mrs. W. F. Wade.

The Reverend J. D. Hudson was retained as pastor. He divided his ministerial duties between the Guemes Church and the Pilgrim Congregational Church in Anacortes..

In 1917, John Kidd offered to sell a half acre of land near the community hall for a church building for the sum of forty dollars. The offer was accepted. The Ladies Aid gave twenty dollars, the W.C.T.U. five and the remainder was collected from church members.

These amounts seem inconsequential today but those years were not easy ones for anyone and money was scarce among Guemes Islanders. At an annual meeting of the church, held October 7, 1917, it was reported that the year's collection had amounted to $18.85. The pastor had other things (probably produce) given him from Guemes to bring the amount to $50.00 for the year.

During depression years, the Ladies Aid sold food at "bake sales." Two such affairs brought the sum of $10.70. The proceeds were used to pay transportation on an organ and some chairs donated by Bellingham friends. At one time the pastor and his wife accepted a quilt made by the Ladies Aid in lieu of part of salary due.

Finally, in 1920, a completed church building was dedicated. Dr. Baird, District Superintendent of Missions, gave the sermon. The church was "packed to the doors." Grace Lincoln Burnham, of Anacortes, was soloist. The Rogers family sang a quartet with violin accompaniment by Vinton Rogers.

The cost of the building, including the fee of Mr. C. H. Kuehnoel, carpenter, was $1,334.69. Sometime later, the Ladies Aid added a kitchen. This brought the total for the church and furnishings to $1,620.00.

During the following years, intermittent improvements have been made. Walls and ceiling of the building have been tiled and the Gertrude Magill Fellowship room, an addition to the church, has been constructed. Mrs. Magill, a charter member, wrote the minutes for church- records for many years. Her final notes in the ledger were dated December 19, 1928. She wrote them during failing health.

Gertrude Magill had been a vital part of the effort made by the few Guemes Islanders to secure a church for the community. During many discussions as to how to finance the project and to develop related problems, Gertrude Magill, with her strong, pioneer spirit, encouraged everyone. She quoted—

> "Bite off more than you can chew and chew it,
> Plan on more than you can do and do it.
> Hitch your wagon to a star,
> Keep your seat and there you are!"

Mr. and Mrs. George Humble, of Guemes, owned the land

between the church and the community hall and when they presented it as a gift to the church the area became the center of religious and social and business concern of the island.

Today—and since 1964, the church is known as The Guemes Island Congregational Church. Men of all faiths are welcome there.

Since its beginning, several ministers have served the church, each in turn. All have shown their vicariate between the Guemes Church and the Pilgrim Church in Anacortes. Today, the pastor for both churches is the Reverend Norman Scruton who lives with his wife, Marion, on the shore of Fidalgo Island. Each Sunday morning this minister crosses the channel on the ferry from Anacortes at nine o'clock, preaches in the Guemes church and returns at ten thirty o'clock to give his sermon in the Pilgrim Church. Each Wednesday he comes again to Guemes to visit with island parishioners and to have lunch with the quilting members of the Women's Fellowship in the church kitchen. At such a time, the Reverend Scruton is known as "Norman." The hours spent with him then as a friend and as he speaks each Sunday morning as a pastor from his pulpit in the little Guemes Congregational Church, are cherished hours for all who know him.

The Women's Fellowship of today, continuing the work of the Ladies Aid of an earlier time, has contributed each year to the need and welfare of the church. When the Magill room was added, through the sale of quilts, their donation was close to one thousand dollars. Liberal monetary gifts from church members, along with funds from the Fellowship also made possible the large modern church kitchen. The fellowship sponsors bake and rummage sales, an art tea and exhibit each year and, at intervals, when there is a church wedding, takes charge of the reception for the bride's family. Also, for large family reunions on the island, the Fellowship has planned and served luncheons. All of this makes it possible to contribute to the church and other worthy causes.

A "quilting bee" today is a rare thing and quilting, in its way, is a fine art. Because of its experienced handiwork, the Women's Fellowship of the Guemes Church has found fame in many places. Quilt tops have come from India, Philippine Islands, Hawaii, France and various sections of the United States. After their designs have been drawn the quilters begin their work. When a quilt is finished it is returned to its owner. Many a home, near and far, displays, with pleasure, its quilt which was once part of a "quilting bee" on Guemes Island.

CHAPTER NINE

IF AN EARLY pioneer on Guemes wanted to get across the channel to Fidalgo Island he went, as his records have confirmed, to the landing near Mangan's dock, got into a small boat and rowed. If there was no wind and the water was calm, this was not too difficult a task. But when the tides ran strong there was danger and a man had to know how to maneuver. Later on, when he acquired a motor and attached it to his small craft, the trip was no longer a laborious pull. Sometimes, too, the pioneer was able to board one of the little ocean going ships which came, periodically, to bring supplies to Guemes, then go on its way to Fidalgo.

When Anacortes was in the process of growing to be a town, the channel crossing became less of a difficulty for the pioneer. A group of men had built the "scow ferry" whose schedule was frequent enough to accommodate the early settler on Guemes.

In 1917 the small ferry "Guemes" came into the lives of those who were residents of the island for which it was named.

Bill Bessner, of Anacortes, knows more about this boat than anyone, and following is an article signed by him.

"The Ferry Guemes…

Built in 1917 by an Everett house carpenter on the beach where the Anacortes Laundry Building now stands. Finished at Keisling Shipyard (now Pacific Towboat). 4 cylinder Atlas built in San Francisco for this specific job-financed and operated by the Guemes Ferry Company which consisted of stockholders from both Anacortes and Guemes Island until 1919 when the company declared bankruptcy. (the treasurer absconded with the funds). Sold at Sherffs sale to Jack Kidd, Bill Alverson and Sol Schreiver for amount of their mortgage. Operated by these men until late summer of 1920 when laid up on beach of Guemes.

Bill Bessner hired in fall of 1920 to put engine back in operating condition. Jacobson hired to overhaul hull. Never had been copper-painted-scraped out terradoes and rot and filled the empty places with cement. Engine frozen—engine room having been full of water. Bill hired to run ferry for owners and did so through 1921. Bought company 1 January 1922. Moved passenger cabin making 6 car ferry in 1927—replaced original engine with diesel Fairbanks approximately 1935.

First fares—50¢ car and driver—passenger free. County subsidize $175.00 per month. Milk cans 10¢ each. First passes issued 1935-$5.00 per car annually with limit one trip daily. In 1929 hauled approximately 400 WPA men working on Guemes roads free daily. Coast Guard allowed 182 adult passengers plus 10% children. The Coast Guard never inspected hull during years Bessner owned the Guemes.

Beached the boat on Guemes to copper-paint. Scrub, scrape and paint one side on low tide one day and the other side the next. Always overhauled engine between last run at night and first run in the morning.

Always had to blindfold some horses to keep them quiet on crossings. Rasmus Hansen angry when Bill started charging 5¢ for foot passengers and rowed from that day on. Frank Wright 1st captain, Chas. Dunn, a stockholder, the second. (Les Dunn has his grandfather's Master's Certificate hanging on the wall in

his cabin on Potlatch Beach.)
        Bill Bessner."

One of those who drove her horses and wagon onto the deck of Bill Bessner's "Guemes" was Jennie Pinneo. This was a valiant lady who lived with her husband Fred and their family on a farm in a beautiful valley on Guemes. Jennie had been crippled since childhood. She used crutches when walking but this did not deter her from working on the farm or taking her cans of milk to market across the channel.

On a certain morning Jennie drove her team with wagon and contents aboard the ferry. Because of the restlessness of the horses the wagon slipped off the boat astern and hung suspended. jennie~s milk cans slid off the wagon an into a watery grave. But she and her horses, aided by the strong arms of the ferrymen and some passengers, clung to life aboard the Guemes. The wagon was hauled to its place on the deck and, later, in Anacortes, Jennie bought some new milk cans and the next day she was back on the ferry, team, wagon, milk cans and crutches on her way to market.

By the year 1948, the county subsidy had increased but Bill had to maintain both boat and dock. His charges were 100 for foot passengers, 750 for car and driver, round trip. Horses and wagons had passed from the scene and Jennie Pinneo now drove her milk cans aboard the ferry in a truck.

For twenty-eight years the "Guemes" had served islanders under the command of its captain, Bill Bessner. When he decided to sell the ferry, those who knew him so well and who had been his passengers under his care for so long, were sad to have him leave. He had their friendship and their respect. When the Guemes brought her last cargo to the island under Captain

Bessner there were many island residents at the dock to say fare-well to the master who had piloted her back and forth across Guemes Channel for many a year.

The Guemes changed hands twice within two years and in 1950 was purchased by Sandrup Bernsen. He kept her in service between Anacortes and Guemes Island for nine years.

During those years Captain Bernsen helped many an island-er in distress, bringing medical help in time of illness or carrying sick patients from Guemes to Anacortes for hospital treatment. He did this without cost for these special crossings.

During an interview with Wallie Funk for the American Bulletin in 1950, Captain Bernsen told of rescuing two instruc-tors from Secret Harbor farms from drowning. Their boat had capsized in Guemes Channel and the ferry went from her usual route and pulled them to her deck. At the time of the South Beach murder the boat brought the captured murderer back to witness the scene of his crime and also, carried the victim across the channel to his waiting relatives. Captain Bemsen said he had ferried wedding parties, picknickers, youngsters, oldsters— "everything."

By 1959 the Guemes had served, altogether, forty two years. Captain Bernsen felt she had labored long enough. And, too, he needed a larger boat.

The Guemes was beached. Charlie Stapp, a Guemes island resident, spoke for many when he admitted having a lump in his throat and when he said: "I am glad to see improved service for the island but, again, I am sorry to see the little boat go."

The Guemes did not rest for long, however. She was purchased by Frank Green and converted into a purse seiner. With her he cruised the open sea. Later, she was destined to run aground on Lummi Rocks in Hale's Passage. No more ploughing through the great water for her. Only the beat of its eternal restlessness upon her enfeebled hull.

The Almar came to Anacortes from the Columbia river. She had been reconditioned so as to be ready for the sea rather than river duty. Three fishermen brought her from Astoria in thirty two hours. She was the property of George Bacon and a group of Guemes Island residents. Captain Bernsen would be the master of the ferry and she would have a crew of two. At that time she was considered a twelve car ferry but, as many cars increased in size, her load would be ten cars or the equivalent.

Slips at Anacortes and Guemes terminals had to be widened some twenty-five feet before they could berth the Almar. Then, when loaded, she crossed the channel for the first time, her bow proved too high above the dock to permit disembarkation. The American Bulletin wrote, apparently with loyalty and pride— "After several tries, the Almar unloaded passengers and took the cars back. Out of the wings, gallantly, came the old ferry (Guemes) and took over for her glamorous successor."

On her second crossing the Almar docked successfully and she has been on duty ever since having served the people of Guemes, thus far, for thirteen years.

Captain Bemsen left as master of the Almar in 1965, when she was taken over by the county. Again Guemes Island felt the loss of a man who had been with them on the ferry during summer mildness and the stormy days of winter and had proven his worth as a friend and as a man of the sea.

Guemes Islanders are aware that the Almar is the property of Skagit County. They know that it is the composite of metal and wood. But, secretly, they ignore its ownership and its content. To them it is not entirely a man made thing. It has a personality. It is an inanimate object which, somehow, through association and necessity, has made itself an integral part of their lives as islanders.

As for the men who bring the Almar back and forth across Guemes Channel—the crew—they are employees of Skagit County. But Guemes islanders have surely and quietly appropriated them along with the ferry. They belong to Guemes though they are residents of Anacortes. Al, Ray, Bob, Russ, Dave, and any other deck man who happens along during a busy season. Our ferry—our ferrymen, Guemes says, with conviction.

Al Bacetich is master of the Almar. His first alternate is Ray Separovich. These two men are cousins. Their families came from Dalmatia, off the coast of Yugoslavia in the Adriatic. They are second generation of their kind in Anacortes. What drew these men to the sea, the navigation of a craft on a waterway of Puget Sound? Heredity, perhaps, for Dalmatia has its need for ships and for seafarers, as well. Bob Leatherwood, second alternate on the Almar is a native of Anacortes. His family has a summer home on Guemes and as for Guemes residents, Bob belongs, ferry, summer home and all, undeniably to the island.

Al, Ray and Bob pilot the ferry. Russ Hauber and Dave Collier are the deck men who steer passengers and cars safely on and off the Almar.

The Almar schedule is from six-thirty A.M. until six o'clock P.M. Monday through Thursday, six-thirty A.M. until midnight on Fridays, seven A.M. until midnight on Saturdays. On Sunday morning the first crossing from Anacortes is at nine o'clock, the last from Guemes at seven in the evening. Extra trips are made if all waiting cars on both sides of the channel cannot be accommodated on the first trips at various hours. After the last evening ferry the residents are on the island for the night.

In case of an emergency on Guemes the police department in

Anacortes is notified by telephone. The police get in touch with the ferrymen who rush to the dock to board the Almar which crosses the channel without delay. If medical care is needed, the police alert the Island Hospital in Anacortes and an ambulance is driven at once to await the return of the Almar with its passenger in need. All of this is accomplished in no more time than such an event would require in a city.

Waiting for the Almar for its ordinary daily runs, especially in fair weather, is a sociable occasion. Cars park in the waiting line and drivers sight friends who are also there to board the ferry. Small groups get together and the latest news of Guemes is started along the grapevine. Andy and Sigrid took off for Washington, D.C., this morning-back in about two weeks. Rollie found over a hundred agates on South Beach yesterday—Alan is getting ready to cut hay for the Black Angus herd—Mary Bohn found an obsidian spearhead where the Indian Village used to be—Evan went fishing to that place way up north—Verna and Phil are due back from Hawaii tomorrow—Two deer, a buck and a doe, swam across Bellingham Channel yesterday and came ashore on West Beach. Mickey is readying to leave for Alaska to work for the summer. Somehow, George's cattle got out of the pasture, there near the dock, and it took two hours to get them in again. Be sure and come to the monthly potluck supper this Thursday. And, have you heard there's talk of the Almar being on dry dock for a couple of weeks overhaul?

This last bit of information strikes horror within the hearts of Guemes islanders for there is no market on Guemes. A little launch is made available, when the Almar is away, for school children and other foot passengers. But it is difficult to get from the dock to Anacortes shopping centers and home again, laden with necessities. Cars are all in Guemes garages. However, somehow,

Guemes hurries and lays in big supplies, enough to last until everything is normal again and life on Guemes is never normal without the little ferry.

Al and his crew always know about Guemes. They know who is home on the island and who has gone east of the mountains to visit relatives. They know who came to Guemes for clamming and who took smoked salmon as a gift to friends in Wichita. If an unwarranted incident occurs they are aware of it and if there is need for an officer of the law they see that he gets to Guemes without delay. Passengers have a way of confiding in the men of the Almar crew. But, sometimes, they know some things without having been told.

A Guemes lady left on an early ferry for a trip to Orcas Island. It was unanticipated and she was certain she hadn't told anyone she was going. During the day her brother and wife from Oregon lined up on the Anacortes dock. They had been in Yellowstone and were returning home and expected to spend the day on Guemes as a surprise visit. A ferryman recognized them and asked — "You aren't crossing to visit your sister are you?" The brother replied that they were and was told that the sister had gone to Orcas for the day and wouldn't be home until time for the last ferry for Guemes. The brother and wife got out of line and went their way to Oregon. The sister didn't know they had tried to visit her until they wrote her a letter and she still doesn't know how the ferryman knew she had gone to Orcas.

Beside the regular ferry crew, Al employs two overseers. He pays them not with county money but with produce just as the pioneers did before they had any money to spend. The produce Al uses comes from his homemade lunches he takes with him to the ferry office on the Anacortes dock. The two overseers have names— Joe and Josephine. No one but Al can tell which is which.

Joe and Josephine are fine looking specimens of the gull world which proves that they thrive, not alone on shell fish but on Al's produce, as well.

When the Almar prepares for a crossing from Anacortes to Guemes, Joe and Josephine fly to the forward bulkhead on the port side. From this high place they gaze upon cars and passengers as the loading is completed. They keep an eye on Al, Ray or Bob, whoever is in the pilot house, knowing that a departure whistle will soon blow and the boat will leave the dock and be on its way across the channel. The passengers know this, too, but they forget about it as they visit with friends on board, lose themselves in the pages of a book or dream as they look over the water, seeing the snow covered summit of Mount Baker.

The blast comes. The passengers are at once in temporary shock, helpless and completely unnerved. But Joe and Josephine don't turn a feather. Only the expected happened as far as they were concerned. Why be thrown off balance?

They fasten a stony gull stare upon the recovering passengers. An enigma, those humans, to Joe and Josephine, a silly lot, all of them—except, of course, Al and Ray and Bob and Russ and Dave.

To the permanent residents of Guemes, the ferry and her crew mean security, the answer to their welfare and their need.

To those seasonal residents or those who plan only a summer day on Guemes the Almar is indispensable. She makes possible their coming and their going.

CHAPTER TEN

GUEMES RESIDENTS, from the earliest pioneer, had peered through darkness by the light of a swinging lantern which they carried in their hands as they walked or by the flickering flame from the wick of a kerosene lamp,

Two island men, "Doc" Finley and John Irvine, wanted electricity for Guemes. Doc was an electrician having had experience in this line of work before he came to the island to live. The two men, Doc and John, in 1948, formed a utility company and incorporated it. At the same time the Guemes Island Cooperative Association, constituted to work in conjunction with the utility company, acquired money through sale of stock in the amount of $24,000. Doc Finley became president of the utility company, John Irvine and his wife vice president and secretary, respectively. Allan Veal headed the cooperative association. Walter Vonnegut, Joe St. Andre, Les Leveque, Charles Townsend, C. L. Versaw and Mrs. R. O. Clippinger were elected as trustees.

The project began May 27, 1948, and for one year Doc and John, together, did the electrical and technical work and the installation for the lighting system on Guemes, fortified by financial assistance from the cooperative association. A year from the starting day, on May 27, 1949, the project was finished.

This was cause for celebration by Guemes islanders and friends across the channel. A banquet featuring strawberry shortcake was planned. It would take place in the Community Hall. Special ferry trips would bring guests and an Hawaiian orchestra from Fidalgo Island. There would be speeches by prominent citizens and by Puget Sound Power and Light officials who had played a part in the laying of a 5,000 foot cable across the channel from Anacortes. There would be dancing after the banquet.

But the unforgettable moment of all, that evening in the Community Hall, came when Doc Finley realized the fulfillment of a dream and turned the switch which brought bright lights to Guemes.

During the days following Guemes women, tired of cleaning chimneys and kerosene lamps, gathered these former necessities and banished them to a junk pile. Jane Veal, wife of president Allan Veal, overcome with joy and enthusiasm, threw her lamps down an old well on on their farm. Now-as she looks backward-Jane wishes she had kept them. Today-and tomorrow-they would be' antiques. Yesterday they had been a burden.

The Lummi Indians taught Bill Fast, a former Guemes resident, their way of barbecuing salmon. Bill taught a P.T.A. group on Guemes, in 1951.

This first barbecue started a tradition on the island, one which was to grow in size year after year until to day the Guemes Salmon Barbecue, held the Sunday before Labor Day, is an event to which hundreds of people come, some from homes many a mile from Guemes Island.

The P.T.A. members, parents of young children, along with the teacher, Walter Vonnegut, wanted playground equipment for the island school. They decided that a quick way to get necessary funds was by giving a salmon barbecue—Lummi Indian style. To complete the meal, Guemes women made salads, pies, cakes and coffee. The men gathered driftwood for the fire and planks for the fish. The salmon were filleted and salted the night previous to the feast.

This first barbecue was held out of doors on South Beach. It was a financial success and the P.T.A. was able to equip the school playground and also help support an island kindergarten with the proceeds.

Within a few years the P.T.A. needed assistance from the Community Club. The two organizations shared the money they made, working together. For several years thereafter the barbecue was sponsored by the club alone and, more recently, has had help from the men of the Guemes Volunteer Fire Department.

A deluge on barbecue day took the event under cover, inside the Community Hall, with the salmon pit and racks outside, south of the building. Here the affair has been held since 1954.

Bill Fast acted as chef until he moved away from Guemes. Walter Vonnegut took his place for a time. At present, various Guemes islanders work together, each one doing his best the task to which he has been assigned. The members of the Guemes Women's Club provide a "Country Store" as part of the barbecue celebration. Homemade pies, bread, cakes, jams and jellies and salads, needlework and handicraft are sold, along with the famous Guemes cook book. Most of the money made in the Country Store is given to the Community Club to augment what is cleared by the barbecue. Fresh fruit and vegetables also bring in a fund as do homemade pie sold as dessert.

As many as seven hundred people have been served at a Guemes barbecue. A taxi service is maintained to bring non islanders from the ferry dock and take them back again when they are ready to board the Almar and pick up their cars on the Anacortes side.

Here is the recipe for barbecuing the salmon, Lummi Indian style, as done on Guemes Island:—

"Bar-B-Q Salmon
Filet salmon and nail the sides on a slab of beach drift, nails about 131 inches apart.

Skin side of fish toward the board and nails driven into the wood only far enough to hold firmly but so that they may be pulled easily after cooling. Then sprinkle generously with rock salt. Store where the draining will not damage anything for exactly eleven hours, then rinse salt off with fresh water.

Now the fish is ready to cook. Build rock and fire pit so that board may be leaned on rack very nearly vertical about 18 inches from the fire.

Use wood for fire with no pitch and no cedar. Keep fire very low so that the juices of the fish are not cooked out. If the juice starts to run down the board cut the fire down or move the fish away. Turn board end for end occasionally. It should take about three hours to cook if it is a large fish or about two hours for smaller size."

The first one room school house built above the south shore by the pioneers was, eventually, too small to accommodate the growing number of children on the island. When the larger school was built on down about two miles from the landing on central Guemes, the P.T.A. which had started the barbecue and fostered many activities to raise funds, continued its work.

With the passing of years, parents of young Guemes children felt that the Guemes school had a too limited curriculum and that Anacortes could offer a broader education. A decision was made to close the island school. This was done in the early sixties and from that time on each morning during the school year a bus has taken pupils from Guemes, by ferry, across to Anacortes where there is a well established educational system. At day's end the children return by bus to their Guemes homes.

The story of the reaction of a small boy to the closing of the Guemes school is still told by islanders.

He was only six or seven, just a little fellow, but he enjoyed his familiar routine. He didn't want the doors of the country school to shut against him and he didn't want to go to school in Anacortes.

"I won't go! I won't go! I won't go!"

What finally brought him to consent could have been one of many things. Even then, he compromised.

"All right!" he said, "I'll go!

But I ain't gonna do no damned work!"

CHAPTER ELEVEN

IN OUR WORLD, among the multitudes, are those to whom Life has brought the gift of diversified talent. An artist, a sculptor, writer, teacher, philosopher, all in one, brings wonder to the hearts and minds of fellowman.

Such a person was Harold Wave Whicker. His friends called him Whick. In the beginning, he and his wife, Meta came to Guemes for holidays. They rented a log cabin above North Beach, and, in 1945 when they decided to make Guemes their permanent home, they moved into this cabin which during their years together was more, much more, to them than a dwelling made of logs.

It was more because Whick with all of his cleverness and capability and Meta with her great gift of perception and understanding knew the true from the false, the pure from the dross. These were the qualities which brought to them the priceless attribute of friendship.

Whick and Meta, who so coveted their association with the Kingston family, George, Sarah and "Dutch," the son who gave his young life in war, had two neighbors across the North Beach road. Tony and Charley, they were, men whose lives became entwined with those of Whick, his wife and the log cabin.

Whick tells it this way, and, in the telling, portrays a part of the down to earth history of the island of Guemes:

"A perennially active youth of eighty-two at this writing,
Tony is usually combing beach with some child at his heels, or
pottering around in his garden or taking leisure on his lawn just
across the road or poking about in that strange shop of his where
I've never failed to find anything needed in routine or emergency. Were the necessity to arise, from his shop, no bigger than
a hatbox, Tony could re-equip and implement heaven and hell
both.

Tony's ancestry is Swiss. The Swiss still shades his speech.
His habitual conversational prelude is this: "Shucks, now you
take back in Wisconsin when I was a kid. . . ." He grew up in the
north woods of that state when it still had frontier hamlets.

Tony's school was not a thing of walls, desks, and a bell. It
was people, Chippewa or white, French-Canadian lumberjack,
German stump farmer or Scandinavian dairyman. Back when
his britches were of no great moment, Tony had something in
him which drew him to people there, and people to him. The
drowse of fireplace embers upon him, Tony will softly drawl of
his first wages as a logging-camp flunkey, nine dollars a month-
this when the snow was three feet deep, the thermometer thirty
below, and the logs coming out of the
          forest on sledges drawn by oxen. He will softly drawl of his
first job in a Great Northern roundhouse, how it led to firing
some old woodburner on a branch line, how this led to the
locomotive engineer's responsibility at the throttle. And while
the embers settle into ashes, his drawl will tell of how he married the "Missus" and brought her out to the sunset when most
coastal towns outside of Seattle were sprawling lumber villages
and Puget Sound mosquito fleet ports in their first thriving off
the salmon. For years Tony was engineer on a Great Northern
branch out of Anacortes up the swift, wild Skagit to Rockport,

a village nestled in Douglas fir forest near the first glacial fringes of the Cascades ... not to know Tony was to pass as a rank outsider. Hitler was taking over the Sudetan and Czechoslovakia when Tony retired. Today, the Great Northern is Tony's heaven with a mountain goat emblematic on its gates of steel, and Jim Hill, who often shook his hand, is his Jehovah.

Long before the ferry began crossing the channel Tony would row over to North Beach of this island. Beach property and land could be had almost for taking possession of it and having a deed recorded.... Tony toppled the great fir trees and blasted out their tenacious roots and stumps.... Like something out of a Swiss village, his cottage grew as Topsy grew. An occasional stump, maybe fifteen feet high, had its reprieve from Tony's dynamite. Upon this stump, reached by a rustic ladder, Tony would build a child's playhouse ideal for home-making and a family of dolls.

Swings hung waiting for children from any bough.

Flanked by bird baths and strange benches made from freak drift of the sea, there was a tiny lagoon where goldfish flashed and swam. Tony's Place, for that is the name it still goes by, was a paradise for children...

Tony was always making things, seldom for himself. Chippewa baskets of cedar bark, reminiscent of his Wisconsin boyhood, rustic chairs, benches, tables, mops, wheelbarrows, quaint practical things out of his own ingenuity and combings from the beach, these. for some neighbor and his wife and their children... Only Tony could create such things. They were never made with deftness and precision of skilled craftsmanship. They had the breath of folklore in them. Indeed, no man ever sensed his way into childhood more completely than did Tony. He is childhood's patron saint. Transplant his shop to the Northland, give him a reindeer or two, and he would run old Kris Kringle out of business. Tony would have been in his element with the Old Woman that Lived in the Shoe.

Tony's garden was God's most prolific spot of earth, a Promised Land of vegetables and fruits and berries and nuts for those around him… It is the nature of the man that wherever he lays his land upon the earth it buds and blooms and yields an incredible abundance and variety to the palate. It is my guess that if he would touch the tip of one of his calloused fingers to a granite rock, that rock would soon be alive with roses and rhododendrons, with daffodils and tulips. I shall always think of him as an emporor over an empire of children and singing birds. I shall always regret that the rulers and diplomats of nations have never had a glimmer of his simple wisdom.

That is the background of Tony's hands and heart.

The background of old Charley's hands and heart is different. Charley spent his early boyhood in Estonia. By the age of twelve he was sailing before the mast. The grand old square-riggers of that day probably winged him to every known port before he was twenty.

The sea, however, was but one of his multiplicity of interests. He could launch into anything, anywhere.… He panned gold in the California gulches. He logged in the California redwood forests. He was in the Yukon gold rush. He turned from prospecting to fishing. He knew Alaska from Nome to Ketchikan; and Alaska knew him, let us have no doubt upon that score.

Then and to the end of his days, for he has had his reckoning with the Dawn, Charlie took life in his own way, and no apologies to God or man. When he held life's cup to his fearless lips, he tossed the hootch there down straight and no shudder upon it afterward.

Even after seventy, Charlie had an iron constitution; and he taxed its metal with all the traffic would bear.

The ladies-God bless them! ... In youth or in age Charley had no more use for a wife than a winged ship has for its anchor when the trade winds are billowing its canvas and careening it on toward far horizons, each of which is forgotten the moment it is in the wake. He spent his money for his pleasure; it was a tempestuous pleasure... He had no more use for bankers than he had for cops in Shanghai and Singapore. When eventually time called him to an accounting of his material assets, he boldly took more whiskey of higher proof and scoffed at the total of his years and taunted them to do their worst. They spewed him up on the Island beach. They left him in a leaky shack, companion of the gulls and cormorants.

It was there that Tony said:

"Shucks, Charley, you and me are friends. I got room on my lot. I'll get the lumber. You build the kind of a place you want."

Old Charley had built the place suggested, a neat two-room cottage on the north end of Tony's lot; and there in peace of mind and all the comfort he desired he let his anchor down for good.... Old Charley's housekeeping was long a subject upon which the community housewives spoke only in whispers; it can best be summed up as a practical working out of the Golden Rule in his relations with the spiders resident of webs thick in any dark corner.

Old Charlie had a cantankerous momma-puss as prolific as the Island soil with Tony's peas.... It was from one of mamma-puss's numerous families that our own Sinbad came...

With tools old Charley was an arch precisionist; he had all the skill of an old guild cabinet worker. He was as exacting as old Tony was un-exacting, as meticulous as Tony was haphazard...

he had the patience of job...

Once he settled down, old Charley did odd jobs and carpentry along the beach... He kept a few chickens.

He never lost his interest in the world at large. He considered the National Geographic, the Readers Digest and a couple of news weeklies necessities second only to whiskey. He read omnivorously... His favorite novels were Tolstoy's War and Peace and Gogol's Dead Souls...Children adored him no less than they adored old Tony...He loved his friends, He hated his enemies.

...In time he welcomed Meta and me into the outspoken warmth of his affection—Meta first, me later; and then we knew, beyond doubt, that we were home.

That is the background of old Charley's hands and heart. There were never better hands. There was never a better heart.

Puget Sound and the roaring tidal turbulence around these San Juans were once known far and wide for their numerous salmon traps. From the weedy shallows, inshore, long rows of piling extended far out to breaks down into depth and held the wire-meshed leads and complexity of webs which often, depending upon location as to spawning runs would imprison tons of Tyee, Coho, Sockeye, Humpbacks, Chum and an occasional giant shark, brown or tiger.

Teredos and other organisms of the sea would eat into the bases of these piling. Billows raised by December gales would smash them off and set them adrift. The tides would strew them along the beaches. For the most part they were beautiful logs, straight as flagpoles, Douglas fir, white cedar or hemlock up to forty, feet in length, a foot to eighteen inches in diameter and permeated with salt water; no land insect would inhabit them.

They needed no barking, no curing in the sun. They were perfect logs for cabin purposes.

It was such logs that old Tony and Charley combed from the beach for this cabin which would be ours...

If only Meta and I could have been there when the cabin was rising! Charlie couldn't work Tony's way. Tony couldn't work Charley's way in anything. When they worked together what suited one never under any circumstances suited the other....

Meta would have laughed herself tearful to see and hear these faithful old friends get into each other's hair over every log grouched into place, over any door or window fitted, over any floor board, over any nail driven and over any brick or stone mortared into that great, cavernous fireplace and chimney.

I do not mean to imply that old Tony and old Charley could get nothing done together. Always they finished what they set out to do; and always that thing done was a blend of their characters and personalities. That, above all, is why Meta and I love this cabin today, why no mansion, however imposing, could ever mean what this cabin means to us. Had I built it, we would have had just another cabin. As it is, our cabin belongs to the folklore and mythology of the Island, for the Island is a place of folklore and mythology...

We make few changes toward the modern, and these, reluctantly. Call it sentiment if you will, but we don't want to rob ourselves of that indefinable something old Tony and old Charley breathed into this stuff of Caesar for us. We want that something on the island long after we are gone. The cabin was all we wanted on earth then. Today we would not trade it for Buckingham Palace."

When Meta and Whick bought the cabin from Tony they told him the price he quoted was not nearly enough.

"Shucks," he drawled, "I don't need the cabin. I need you folks, so we'll let it go at that."

"Whereupon" Whick said, "Sinbad saw fit to purr against the calf of Tony's leg."

Harold Wave Whicker died in June, 1955. As he lived, he had given much of his knowledge as an educator at the Naval Academy in Anapolis, University of Montana and Washington State College. He was a gifted man. Through his written word and his artistry he reflected the wonder of nature. He could evaluate the worth of a man and his accomplishment and, because of his sensitivity, Old Tony and Old Charley walked deep into his heart.

Today, Meta still lives in the log cabin, Whick's water colors hang upon the walls, a piece of his sculpture is here, a book of his writing there. Sometimes, Meta gazes across the county road to the place where Tony and Charley once lived for they are gone, along with Whick and Sinbad.

It was an unforgettable chapter they all wrote, together, on North Beach, Guemes Island.

CHAPTER TWELVE

PHILIP MCCRACKEN, each morning, leaves his Guemes Island home and walks, just a little way down the North Beach road. He opens a gate and enters a garden. The sun, filtering through spreading branches, touches him and the air, he senses, is sweet with the scent of apple blossom. Apple blossom on the trees "Old Tony planted. Phil reaches a house in the garden. He opens the door and enters the place which Tony built with his caloused hands and which, even today, is known to islanders as "Tony's Place." This is Phil's studio.

The charming old two story structure belongs, now, to the McCrackens, Phil and his wife, Anne. Its preservation through normal years is assured, for they treasure its background.

Within its walls there will be creation—Phil is a sculptor and a painter. He is one of the gifted men of Guemes, today.

Philip McCracken was born in Bellingham, Washington, in 1929. Most of his boyhood was spent in Anacortes. He is the son of William McCracken and is third generation of his family here in the Skagit County area.

Phil went from Anacortes High School to the University of Washington in 1947. His college years were interrupted by service in the Army after which he returned to the University and graduated in 1953 from the School of Art. The work of Henry Moore had a strong appeal and Phil wanted to be his pupil. He wrote to the famous English sculptor, sent him a few sketches and asked to be taken as a pupil. Henry Moore accepted him.

The crossing of the Atlantic from America to England brought the romance of the sea. Aboard the ship Phil met Anne MaeFetridge, a New York girl from Mt. Holyoke College with a master's degree from Cornell University. She had planned to teach in England but before long she and Phil were married and Henry Moore was Phil's best man.

Now Phil and Anne have three teenage sons. They live on North Beach overlooking Bellingham Channel. There may be other homes such as theirs but if so, they would be hard to find. Theirs is unique. It is unique because they, themselves, make it so. Their door opens so willingly that many who go through it into the McCracken family room soon have the feeling the home belongs to them. Countless guests have been welcomed around their table. Many a lonely person has found comfort just being, even for a short time, in this home. Many a wounded bird has lived with the McCrackens until its broken wing healed and it was set free to fly once again. Here is a home where books gather no dust upon the shelves. They are read. Prose and poetry are often a topic of conversation-music, classical and modern is played. And watch as you walk in the McCracken home for two huge collies, Girl and Halfmoon, and Maggie, a large white poodle may be sprawled upon the floor. And look before -you sit in the most comfortable chairs or you may disturb the cats, Honey Bear, the long haired one or Ferd, the domestic short hair. No one is ever surprised to see several little furry waifs, found abandoned somewhere, boarding with the McCrackens until they can find a home and someone else, who cares.

Philip McCracken is a nationally known sculptor and paint-er. He shows at the Willard Gallery in New York. One of his sculptured pieces has its place at United Nations. Art collectors, east and west in our country include his work in their galleries. His "Caged Bird" draws' attention in the Seattle Center Theatre. "Mountain Guardian," a bird of prey stands high on a mountain overlooking Fidalgo Island. Phil carved it in memory of someone who wanted it there as an expression of the many happy years he had known, before his life ended, in Anacortes. Phil's sculpture is the focal attraction at entrances of business institutions in Seattle and, on Guemes, if one goes through a forest, along a sheltered road, he will come suddenly in a clearing, upon "Spring" a wooden sculpture of exquisite workmanship which comes from its pedestal as though it were rooted in the earth,. as its budding leaves reach for light from the April sky.

Phil is a perfectionist. As, in sensitivity, he forms a creature of nature, there is indescribable beauty. But he can also create a startling thing which cries from the depth of reality of man, of life, of death and destruction.

Phil can do all of this because his thoughts penetrate his world. Beauty and torment—he reaches out, for both.

Philip McCracken is a compassionate man. He is soft spoken. He is loath to criticize his fellow men. He is gentle. But, he is also strong. It is this strength and the compassion which is a part of him, which emanate from within and bring undeniable refinement, vitality and eloquence to everything he fashions with his gifted, artist hands.

Max Benjamin is another artist of note who makes his home on Guemes Island. He lives at the end of a quiet forest road in a large rustic house which seems to have grown there, a part of natural surroundings. The structure includes, within its walls, a gallery where he hangs some of the forceful and colorful pictures which he paints.

With his wife and four children, Max Benjamin has labored

on his two-hundred acre farm to make of it a thing of beauty-wilderness and cultivated gardens combine to complete the scene which this artist could so well portray upon a canvas. Sometimes, to augment the family income he goes "long-shoreing" when ships anchor at nearby Puget Sound ports.

Max Benjamin was born in San Diego in 1928. He came to Seattle when he was sixteen years of age. Within a few years he went to Europe and visited galleries and museums. He returned to the Northwest, attended the University of Washington where he graduated from the School of Art in 1955. In 1959, after working for Boeing, he moved his family to Guemes Island so that he would have more time for his painting.

Since 1954 Mr. Benjamin has exhibited in the foremost museums and galleries of the Pacific Coast. His paintings have been shown at the Henry Gallery at the University of Washington, Santa Barbara Art Museum, Denver Art Museum, Panaca Gallery, the Capitol Museum in Olympia and others.

Mr. Benjamin has reviewed Art for the Seattle Times newspaper and has taught a number of art classes in his home area.

But, mostly he paints. He has in his own collection his expressionistic landscapes, abstract landscapes, modem objective paintings. Some of his work is so powerful in color and form, with bursting flame and violent action it reaches for the viewer, volcanic proportion.

But, too, Max Benjamin paints a quiet scene of water, earth and sky-a part of the island wilderness which had called to him and to which he had answered and come to make his own.

Sometimes, in the quiet of a Guemes Island evening, Esther Smith plays her violin. With her gift of music, she stirs the souls of her listeners.

Esther Smith, after graduation from college in Kansas,

received her master's from Northwestern University. For many years she was supervisor of music in the Kirkland schools, Washington. She is retired, now, living in her island home on the South shore, overlooking the channel and Anacortes in the background. She rehearses regularly and plays in concert as a member of the Seattle Philharmonic orchestra.

Music has been Esther Smith's forte. She knows her instrument. It answers to every stroke of her bow by her skilled hand upon its strings. Her technique is masterly. For her the violin sings or weeps according to her wish.

To hear, as island twilight falls, the strain of Ave Maria, to feel the poignancy, the purity of tone, is to live a perfect moment. This is the contribution of a violinist, to Guemes.

Linda Porter is the granddaughter of Louis Shoultz, early settler, whose friends referred to as "Old Man Shoultz." She is the niece of Marvin Shoultz, son of Louis, who lives in the house his father built, farms the acres his father cleared from the forest- and grazes cattle on its lush pastures.

Linda lives with her husband Bob on West Beach on Guemes. They were sweethearts at Anacortes High School where Linda gained prominence as a painter. She later studied art at Skagit Valley College and was given the Skagit Art Association scholarship.

Linda is a printmaker. Including wood cuts, zinc engravings and linoleum cuts, her work is that of an expert craftsman.

Linda also designs jewelry, mostly cast in silver.

Louis Shoultz could only feel pride in his granddaughter's progress thus far, as an artist.

If one is a stranger on Guemes and doesn't feel at ease walking in darkness or even in moonlight when shadows come and go, he should not stroll at night on West Beach. He might reach the locale of Liten Lodge.

Should he arrive at this place and turn his eyes from the water of Bellingham Channel toward the island slope he would behold, very close, something weird and altogether frightening. He might even wonder if,, unknowingly he had died and gone to an unknown habitat somewhere in the universe, of fiends and threatening monsters.

He would see huge staring eyes, a water beast, its open jaws and elongated teeth ready for a victim. He would see diverse, unearthly forms ready to sweep him into some sort of eternity.

But, if be should stay until dawn he would lose his fear and dread. For the light of day would tell him that creatures so mysterious at night were only driftwood, shells and rocks.

This is the garden of Liten Lodge—the creation of a Guemes resident known as "Bubbles."

Bubbles, a former Anacortes girl, has spent years of her life collecting odd pieces of driftwood. She has made of them, in her garden, the semblance of birds and animals as well as nameless illusions of her own fantasy. A driftwood ostrich wears a necklace of clamshells and uses one for an eye. A creature whose like has never been seen before, and probably never will be again, stands beside a cabin door, bedecked in clam shells and, appears, as one attempts to read his empty countenance, his huge nose and his open mouth, to be wondering how he ever got there.

There are starfish, sea urchins, various shell fish-all fashioned by Bubbles. There is a skull of a mountain sheep or a goat, whichever it may be. Also, there is a totem pole carved from a cedar log by Bubbles, herself.

This Guemes lady has carried the atmosphere of her unusual garden into her unusual home. The facade of her fireplace displays thousands of colorful beach pebbles. Old treasures, from pioneer days are part of the decor of each room. There are, if one is granted a glance into a clothes closet, some dresses once worn by the first ladies of Guemes and Anacortes.

Bubbles has a unique sense of humor. A friend, rather new on Guemes, had tea with her one day. Moving about the house, from one room to another, she opened a door and came face to face with a skeleton hanging against the wall. It was a large skeleton of an adult and its impact sent the friend reeling into the living room. There, she looked toward a window. On its sill was a coiled rattlesnake. Rooted, the friend stood, figuring how she could make it past the snake to the great out of doors without being bitten. It was then that Bubbles laughed. The snake was a lifelike ceramic.

This humor of Bubbles has, no doubt, eased her over many of the exigencies which have, from time to time, come into her life. The originality of her garden which has come from her direction for fantasy has interested many who have walked the west beach of Guemes and come to Liten Lodge.

Agates are everywhere on Guemes beaches, more some places than others, but experienced hunters can always find them. They come in all sizes and many colors, usually soft and delicate in shade. An amber agate is said to be found only on Guemes. The cornelian is deeper in shade than most agates but there is a soft glow which gives it a mellow hue. Adventurine and jasper are also found, jasper cherished for its varied coloring and adventurine because of its translucence.

There are many fine collections of agate and stone on Guemes, all of which have gone through the polishing process and sometimes they are set into jewelry. Agate hunting has proven to be a rewarding and enjoyable hobby for islanders whose lives are leisurely and free of demanding tasks.

CHAPTER THIRTEEN

GUEMES, SOMETIMES, laughs at itself.

When long hair, bushy whiskers, mustaches, sideburns and goatees came into fashion for men, Guemes wasn't ready.

One day a station wagon drove onto the ferry at Anacortes. Its driver had all of these accoutrements in a bright shade of auburn.

The ferry crew looked askance at the newcomer and so did a certain Guemes islander, aboard on his way home. All of that covering might be concealing the face of a decent man or the visage of a wanted criminal.

When the man drove off the ferry he turned on his way along the south shore. The islander followed at a discreet distance and after a few miles he saw the stranger park his wagon at the side of a road in a grassy area under the shade of evergreen trees.

The islander was dubious. He went home and called the Sheriffs office in Anacortes.

"There's a man over here parked in a secluded place. Maybe he's all right, I don't know. He's an odd looking specimen. Can't you send one of your men over? He could just drive along casually and maybe find out what the man is doing on Guemes."

An officer of the law arrived by the next ferry. He found the station wagon, paused beside it and engaged its occupant in conversation-casually, as the islander had suggested. After a mere few minutes he was on his way to catch the next ferry for Anacortes. From the Sheriff's office he telephoned the waiting islander.

"You're safe, all of you people on Guemes," he said, "that poor guy is a well known university professor. He's so tired of being in crowds and noise and a city rat race he just came to Guemes to spend a weekend and get away from it all!"

Guemes Islanders laugh at one another and delight in mock tragedy.

When young Tim McCracken wanted to go on a summer trip to Europe with high school classmates from Anacortes he began thinking of ways to make money to help pay his expenses.

Coming to a conclusion, he bought a little pig and named her Primrose. He hoped in time she might have some little pigs of her own and give him an income.

True to form in the McCracken family, Primrose became a pet. She ran around the garden with members of the dog and cat clan and received her share of attention from the residents of the North Beach area.

But, as time passed, Primrose was no longer a little pig. She put on weight at an amazing rate of speed and it was apparent there wouldn't be much left of anyone's garden if she continued on her way.

Tim found a place for her on a big lot across the road. The property belonged to a neighbor, Dorothy, who was quite willing to have Tim build a pen there and put Primrose inside it.

But Primrose missed her freedom and her petting. She was lonely. Even so, she grew heavier by the day. Tim was searching for the right companion for her the moment Dorothy was bending over, weeding her garden. She heard a sound and turned to

see Primrose leave her pen behind her. Dorothy was her destina-
tion, and Dorothy was terrified. She ran as the wind blows and
made it to the house in time to shut the door against the face of
Primrose.

"Tim! You'll have to take her away from here! She chased
me! She might have knocked me over!"

"Aw!" Tim said. "She just wanted you to pet her."

Just then Dorothy looked toward the garden and saw Primrose devouring some brambles she had been trying to uproot for
years. She mellowed. Primrose stayed. Guemes laughed.

Tim went to Europe. The fate of Primrose after his departure
was not recorded.

Guemes laughed again, recently, when a charming silver
haired lady caused a furor.

On a Sunday morning the congregation of the Guemes
Island Community Church sat in reverent silence waiting for
the pastor, Norman Scruton to arrive after he had crossed on
the nine o'clock ferry from Anacortes. Soon the Arnold Houles
arrived, friends with whom he rides, and everyone knew that
the minister had gone through a side entrance into the church
kitchen to put on his clerical robe. He was expected, within a few
minutes, to enter the inside church door and go to his pulpit to
begin his service.

But this didn't happen. There was no sign of the Reverend
Scruton. The congregation began to fidget. Something was
wrong—he was ill—had he had a stroke? Had he --?

Two Deacons rose from their seats, walked in dignity, side by
side, opened the kitchen door and closed it behind them. What
they saw was a disheveled minister clutching a butcher knife,
struggling to open a "powder room" door. He was a distraught
man with only an hour to deliver his Sunday services, doomed

to rescue a certain parishioner who kept pounding on the inside of the "powder room" door screaming all the while that she was dying of claustrophobia.

The Deacons joined the minister and attacked the broken lock. The captive was freed.

Within the chapel, the congregation had become so frightened it was ready to rush en masse into the kitchen. just at this moment, fortunately the Deacons reappeared, immobile of countenance and went to their waiting seats. The kitchen door opened and the Reverend Scruton, robe flying, speeded to his pulpit. He muttered something about being sorry he had been delayed, opened his Bible, said a prayer of thankfulness and began his sermon. The congregation found time while singing a hymn to recover its equilibrium.

The entrance door of the chapel opened and closed and a charming, silver haired lady found her pew. Her composure was deceitful. The congregation thought she had just arrived from home, late for church that Sunday morning.

When worship had ended, the Deacons could no longer control their pent up hysteria. As the delayed minister went at breakneck haste to catch his ferry and get to his church in Anacortes, the story of the kitchen drama was told.

Before nightfall the grapevine had carried the tale to the four corners of Guemes and Guemes laughed.

Through it all the silver haired parishioner maintained composure and charm, but someone saw her laughing when she didn't know the eye of Guemes was upon her.

Guemes laughs. But she has also come near to weeping.

A few years ago, word came that an organization hoped to construct an aluminum reduction mill on Guemes Island. Offers had been made to certain land owners for their property, offers so attractive they would be difficult to refuse. The part of Guemes the organization planned to buy included one of the most beautiful areas on the island.

Certain Guemes residents felt that industry would be an economic improvement. Others were terrified at the thought of the change it would bring to the quiet, secluded country life they treasured.

The two opinions brought into being two factions. Those who favored the coming of the plant, wanted it badly. Those who did not want it were strong in their resentment against it.

A situation developed which reached explosive proportion. Nerves were taut, friendships suffered.

Permission was granted the plant backers to rezone the island for heavy industry. The dispute reached the Superior Court, then the Supreme Court. At this point the Aluminum Company said the legal process was taking too long and that it had decided to go elsewhere. It left the scene and no word ever reached Guemes as to its establishment in another area. The Supreme Court rendered a decision against the rezoning. Guemes would remain unchanged.

This unhappy affair was, in its way, a normal thing. All men do not desire the same. It would be a dull world if they did.

A few residents, disappointed and disillusioned left Guemes and went elsewhere to live. Those who remained, after the ordeal had ended, had time to measure the worth of the distress they had suffered.

It was not difficult for them, in the aftermath of the island battle to know that someone always wins, someone always loses. It is the way of life. Those on Guemes who had lost this time would win some other struggle as their years go by. And the islanders who won and kept industry from the quietude of the beautiful valley knew that they would some day be the losers for another cause.

Today on Guemes, friends are friends, dissension has been stifled and memories, whatever they may be, have been hidden away as part of a human past.

The permanent population of Guemes today numbers about two hundred and fifty people. It is increased when the "summer residents" arrive to live in their beach cottages. When they come they keep the ferry on a steady run. Their station wagons are laden with baggage, food supply, "kids,", dogs, cats—all ready for a vacation on Guemes. When they leave in early fall, the Almar and her crew settle down for their regular winter schedule.

The Guemes of today is still, partly the Guemes of yesterday.

There are the quilting bees, the pot luck suppers, the barbecue and the Country Store. On Thanksgiving Day "Pilgrims" who want the old way of Plymouth Rock sit around a table together for their turkey dinner in the Guemes Island Community Hall.

The Volunteer Fire Department meets once a month. Over the fire house door, upon a wooden plaque, there is an inscription honoring the memory of a former Guemes resident. It was carved by "J. O." McClung, a Guemes friend. It reads:

> "Robert E. Howard Station.
> Skagit County, F.P.D. No. 17
> Guemes Island."

Young couples are buying and building homes on Guemes. A young man who isn't an architect or a carpenter decides he can construct his own house. He accomplishes this as he works part time to support his family, attends college as he studies for his master's or his doctorate, and the community marvels.

If someone on Guemes has a flat tire or locks his keys in his car, a neighbor helps. If a garage door won't close, a friend sees that it does. So much is done on Guemes by a non-paid worker, someone, here and there, who has learned to give of himself.

Louise Pinneo, widow of George Pinneo, wrote the news of Guemes for an Anacortes newspaper for forty years. She has moved to a nursing home on Fidalgo and she does not write during these latter years of her life but she still is one who volunteers. She comes to Guemes each week to sew at the quilting bee.

The pioneer women of Guemes worked in home and field. This happens today. "Maud Muller on a summer's day raked the meadow sweet with hay" and so does Ruth Johns-and drives a truck besides-to help herself through college. After this day's work is done she rides her horse bare back along the quiet roads of Guemes, for recreation. Many island women mow their lawns and Esther Smith, away from her violin, astounds everyone by driving her tractor, plowing her vegetable garden and repairing mechanical ills usually referred to masculine territory. One Guemes lady-not young, climbed a tall cedar, one the Indians knew, and rescued her kitten from a dizzying height. Another, who has five great grandchildren doesn't bother to go through a gateway. She climbs over a rail fence while down the road "apiece"; neighbors gape from their windows waiting for her to fall.

It's a good life on the island. Always there are diverse opinions as well as agreement and cooperation. World affairs and politics are important to Guemes residents. Their minds are never closed to the outside even though they live within the perimeter of a small San Juan.

The wild rose of summer blooms today on Guemes. Early spring blossoms have come and gone but Scotch broom is golden along the roadsides. In hidden hollows and on remote hill tops the blue camas flower, shadow of Indian days, still grows. The wild cherry is a soft white cloud amid the deep green of the forest. Buttercups cover the meadow land and succor the bees with their honey. A humming bird has two young in her nest near the window of an island home. The flicker is here again and eagles perch in tree tops while the call of a loon comes from the quiet water of the channel. There are the lowing herds in Guemes pastures. A varied thrush sings from the branches of an alder tree. Islanders cannot find words to describe the beauty of the rhododendron. Dogwood and chestnut trees are blossoming. Seagulls fly high and low and steal shell fish from their companions. Crows caw and flee from hawks. And, out of the quietude of the island wilderness, deer come, silently, and gaze, from a distance, in wonder, at the way of mankind.

CHAPTER FOURTEEN

GUEMES, SMALL world of whispering yesterdays—of now—and of infinite years waiting to come, enfold you, then go, leaving the graven memory of their time.

Guemes, small world, clinging to your solid past, let the echo of a larger world as it floats across the waters of Puget Sound, pass you by.

And, if you walk an island road and find a sea of daffodils, golden in the sun, pause to envision the one who placed the first one within your soil, even a hundred years ago.

Think, as you pause, of those who found you, the Indians, nature's children, and the early white settler, asking nothing from any man which he could not repay in labor or in substance.

Think, also, of that pioneer wife who tilled the Guemes soil with her husband-knowing so well the destined pattern of her life. Knowing so well, that when he offered to give her a diamond ring, she spoke these words:

"I think I'd as leave you gave me a cow."

For special and basic facts concerning the Indian people, our early Americans, grateful acknowledgment is given the following: *Vancouver's Discovery of Puget Sound*, Edmond S. Meany; Secretary of State Earl Coe's book, *Indians in Washington; Indians of Puget Sound* by Herman Haberlin and Ema Gunther.

University of Washington Publications; *Indian Tribes of*

Oregon, Washington and Idaho, John R. Swanton; *Sea in the Forest,* Archie Binns; *Pictorial History of the State of Washington,* Ralph Ernest Downie; *The Fourth Corner—Indians of the Northwest,* Lelah Jackson Edson; *Bury My Heart at Wounded Knee,* Dee Brown; *Potlatch,* George Clutesi; *Indian Life on the Northwest Coast of North America,* Ema Gunther; *Indians of the Northwest Coast,* Philip Drucker; *Indians of Skagit County,* Chief Martin J. Sampson.

Quotes from the words of Chief Joseph of the Nez Perce and of Crowfoot of the Blackfoot were taken from "Touch of Earth," a self portrait of Indian Existence, compiled by T. C. McLuhan.

References from the following newspapers: Guemes Tillikum, The Beachcomber, Anacortes Bulletin, Anacortes Daily Mercury, Anacortes American, Seattle Times Pictorial.

GUEMES GLEANINGS

Gertrude Howard

Phone Cable Coming

Island Com
Made New
Re

., TUESDAY, OCT. 22, 1912.

OUR ISLAND OF TODAY

Developing Rapidly Into one of Washington,s Fairest of Home Sites

was never a time since the Guemes Island that has been made resources

CHARLEY L. GANT, Editor and Proprietor.

VOL. I,

OUR EARLY SETTLERS

The Men Who First Chose Guemes Island as a Permanent Home Site.

OLD TIMERS STILL HERE.

Many Changes Since 1862 the Real Beginning of the First Settler's Story.

Many changes have taken place on Guemes Island since the memorable time en a deer represented four dollars

The author, Gertrude Howard and her husband Bob discovered the charm of Guemes Island in the mid 1940's. They became Island boosters from the moment they arrived. The Robert E. Howard Fire Station honors Bob's memory.

Gertie, as Mrs. Howard is affectionately known, became the Guemes Community Club historian since no printed reference to the Island or its inhabitants has she ever allowed to go unnoticed. Her garret attests to the fact that she is a one-woman clipping service.

In 1978 Gertie was asked to prepare this paper from her garret "gleanings." Its purpose was fulfilled when C.P. Stapp embellished it with his memories while reading it for the enjoyment of the Community Club members at one of their meetings. Later, to satisfy requests, the Club agreed to have it printed.

Gertie's "Gleanings" is an unduplicated continuation of the first printed history, Elmore's "The Isle of Guemes" published in 1973. In fact the history of Guemes Island is on going. We can expect further accounts as its devotees record their own memories and experiences.

Sylvia Carothers
President 1976 - 78
Guemes IslandCommunity Club

First printing -1981

It is known that Indians gathered and lived on Guemes before the arrival of white settlers. Kitchen middens have been found on South and West Beach. There was also a large Potlatch house on West Beach. There are conflicting reports as to its size. One report says it was 250 feet long and 35 feet wide, and another says 999 feet long.

The Potlatch was a social function - usually held during the salmon run - with feasting and an exchange of gifts. There was speech making, singing and games, and the men gambled. I have read that the last great Potlatch on Guemes was held in the 1880's; 1884, in fact, when the Anacortes paper stated that… "Great numbers of canoes containing entire families of Indians, the women and girls dressed in the brightest colors, passed Anacortes on their way home from the Potlatch held at their rendezvous on Guemes Island." But then there's another report which states there was a Potlatch there in 1917. [See also The Samish Indians of Guemes Island, 1792-1986]

Guemes Island was discovered by George Vancouver in 1778. An interesting note here: Don Taylor told me he has read Captain Vancouver's log. He, Vancouver - left his anchor by the Yellow Bluffs on Guemes. He was anchored there, the tide was flooding, and it was impossible to get his anchor in.

The name was given to Guemes, though, by the Spanish explorer, Don Francisco Eliza, who named it for a Mexican Viceroy. That was in 1791 or 1792. Guemes was also known as Lawrence Island for a time. And, of course, everyone has heard it called Dog Island.

I have read two different reasons for that name. One is that Henry Roeder and Russell Peabody who, in 1853, had started a lumber mill at Whatcom Falls, were bringing men and supplies in a sloop and stopped over night on Guemes. During the night a pack of wild dogs attacked the camp. These dogs had been left behind to roam and increase when the Indians left the island.

The other version: Before factory-made blankets, the Indians raised a breed of white shaggy dogs that were clipped, and the fur was then used for weaving blankets.

Our island is 7.96 square miles in size, and the highest point is 560 feet.

A man named Hall was the first settler on the island. He stayed long enough to build a small cabin and then left.

Jim Matthews - grandfather of Sarah Kingston and Maude Wooten - settled with his family on Guemes in 1865 and, according to one source, was the builder of the first house on the island. Sarah told me the family was flooded out on the Samish flats, came by boat, and landed on the south shore of Guemes about a mile east of the present ferry dock, where they homesteaded. The Hammill property in that area is part of that homestead.

At that time, Sarah's father was four years old. A sidelight - George Kingston told me that when the Matthews ran short of water in the summertime they would take their dirty clothes to the springs area on the southeast, build a fire to heat the water, and do their laundry there. Sarah's mother practiced folk medicine. She mixed natural ingredients such as roots from Oregon grape, licorice fern, etc. She cured one neighbor of consumption.

Humphrey O'Bryant settled on Guemes in 1866. He planted a large orchard of 400 apple trees and 225 prune trees. Ed Donnelly, who now owns the old homestead, told me that Mr. O'Bryant went by canoe to Victoria to personally pick out his trees. Humphrey O'Bryant is buried out on the point of the property he owned.

Timothy Mangan arrived in 1871. He built the first store in 1873. He established a small lumber yard, and he built the first dock. The first white child born on Guemes was born to the Mangans. The earliest dances were held in the Mangan kitchen, and later in his store. Nate Lewis and Louis Shoultz both played violins, and the Mangans had a small pump organ. In the winter the young people rode to the dances in a sled drawn by oxen. T.B. Mangan was elected Justice of the Peace in 1883.

John Shriver also came to Guemes in 1871 and took up a homestead. He lived here until 1918, when he died at 85. Two of his brothers were also Guemes pioneers - Sol and Jake. Jake was the grandfather of Sadie (Mrs. Horace) Hammill. Their homestead took in the area that is now Ocean Acres and the Hammill place.

Bill Payne was also an 1871 arrival. He took up a pre-emption claim which had belonged to that first settler, Hall. That farm was sold years later to the Bessner family, and he then built the house which is now just a shell on South Shore Drive. There is a story that he donated the North Beach Park to the people of Guemes, but that isn't really so. When he died at age 79 in 1923, his heirs sold that land to the City of Anacortes for $275.00.

Lucius Blackinton came to Guemes in 1872. He had 160 acres on South Beach. He owned a store, and was appointed the first postmaster on the island in 1890. After three years there came a crash, and that ended the post office. During that period, there were about 100 people on Guemes. The store and post office were in a building that is now part of the Elden Palmer home. The building was moved up from the beach. Blackinton planted that large and lovely beech tree in the Benjestorf yard.

John Edens arrived in 1872. He was joined by three brothers and they built up a logging business that lasted several years. Oxen were used for logging at that time, and the Edens employed as few as ten and as many as twenty-four men. The

Edens, of course, donated the school ground as well as most of the land for the cemetery. Their homestead was the area we now call The Hollow.

I am unable to pinpoint the exact year that Nathan Lewis and his wife, Florence, arrived. There are several dates given, but my guess would be that it was in the mid-1870's. He built his house where Butch Kreiger now lives; however, Butch's house is the second Lewis House. The first one burned. Mr. Lewis owned a great deal of the North Beach property at one time. Mrs. Lewis named their place Maplewood Farm. Like the other pioneers of these first years, they rowed to LaConner for necessary supplies, and when they were in need of a doctor.

Another settler in the 1870's was Lawrence "Smuggler" Kelly whose story has been told many times. His cabin was half way up the bluff on Kelly Point. For twenty-five years he smuggled Chinese laborers from Canada for as much as $500 per head. He also smuggled opium and some wool. He was arrested and fined many times. He even served time for his illegal deeds, but always came back to smuggle another day. His last days were spent in a home for Confederate Veterans.

Some of the other names in the early history of Guemes were Martin Wilfong, whose wife was the first white woman on the island; Amos Johnson, whose disappearance and murder caused quite a stir; William Whaley; C.P. Woodcock and James Murrow. And a very prominent early Guemes name is Causland. Mr. and Mrs. Causland arrived on the island in the mid-1880's and took over a homestead - the land that is now the Veal farm. For the story about how the lumber and brick were acquired and brought to the site, read Helen Elmore's "This Isle of Guemes".

In the very early days the settlers were busy clearing land and building homes. Logging and shingle-making were the sources of income for some time.

There was also a "go" at mining. The first mention of such activity was in 1876 when a copper mine was opened. Tunnels were dug several hundred feet into the mountain, but there are no records of actual production. There was a write-up about reopening this mine in 1884 but, again, nothing about actual mine production. The mine was located not far from the waterfront on the H.P. O'Bryant place. There were talc deposits on Cooks Bay, and an excellent grade of Potters clay was found on the island. There was, supposedly, even a gold mine which, according to one oldtimer, was "salted" to sell shares.

In about 1909 the island was well into becoming a farming community. The forests had been cleared and the soil was fertile. By 1912 farming was a serious business. The orchards that had been planted some years earlier produced good quality fruit. Excellent berries and vegetables were grown, and there were a number of dairy and poultry farms. Charles Gant wrote in his paper about potatoes weighing one pound each, three onions adding up to four and one-half pounds, and plums that would make duck eggs look like Tom Thumb peas.

Before coming to Guemes Island, Charley Gant worked on papers in Bellingham, Mount Vernon and Anacortes. Before that in about 1901 - he published a paper in the Grays Harbor area that he called "Gant's Sawyer." Charley himself admitted in his writings that he was addicted to the Demon Rum, but somehow that didn't affect those writings. He had an astute command of the English language and a beautiful way with words. He was a natural poet, and his writings seemed to come out in rhyme, whether intended or not. Charley loved Guemes and wrote many verses about the island and its people.

The first paper on Guemes was the "Tillikum." Lee Lewis

was the publisher and Charley Gant the editor. The first issue was dated April 8, 1912. The "Tillikum" was written and printed on North Beach. The partnership of Lewis and Gant lasted until the following February when Charley really fell off the wagon and went on a destructive spree. On February 14, 1913, he became sole owner of the "Tillikum." Lee Lewis left the island to go to work on a steamboat in Tacoma. It was at that time this column appeared in the paper: "There is no use wasting your time roasting the Editor of the "Tillikum ", my dear. Just go right on with your quilting and knitting, sweetheart, and let us tell you what a disreputable, baldheaded old beast we are when we go sauntering down the road to hell arm-in-arm with John Barleycorn. We have been both up and both down the sunny and shady sides of life, yet the only reflection we have ever seen of life's other side came the other day. We looked into the mirror. Sorry looking sight, honey, beautiful brown eyes all red with rum, and intellectual brow all wrinkled like an old maid's convention. Yes, we are a degenerate son of a drunken sire, darling, good at times, and bad between times. But don't waste your time in roasting us, dovey - we are not worth your while. Just go ahead with your knitting." Some weeks following that, the "Tillikum" came to an end.

But Charley came back in 1916 as the sole owner of the "Beachcomber." His first office was in the vicinity of the shipyard location. Later, he moved to a building east of the ferry dock and across the road from where Bud Hanson now lives. This office must have been fairly large dances were held there. The "Beachcomber" was published for about seven years. When Charley Gant died in Bellingham, he was 67 years old. A book is being written about Charley, and will be published this summer.

In the early spring of 1912, N.B. Lewis cleared and beautified land on North Beach and called it Idlewild Park - a resort park with room for about 100 tents. It was very popular because it had the warmest bathing beach on the island. This was because the smooth bottom and the shallow tides received the warm sun the entire day. By May of 1917, there were two-roomed summer cottages for rent.

That same summer - 1912 - Henry Howard established a similar spot on South Beach, which he called Kentucky Treat. He put in foundations and floors for tents, and families from off the island located there for the summer. There was a place for large picnics too, with contests, foot races, tug of wars and baseball.

Paul Jones Park came into being on South Beach in 1923. It was also a place for picnics, baseball games and 4th of July celebrations.

The women of the island organized a Social Club in February 1912 with twenty-five charter members. The club was formed for the purpose of raising money to build a social hall. They were a great group of, "go-getters". They raised money by having bazaars, lunches, dinners, dances, ice cream socials, box suppers, etc. They pieced and raffled quilts. Their dances were sometimes advertised by putting notices on slides at the Rose Theater in town. The money-raising process, though, was slow. By June 1913, they had $104.50 in their treasury. Again, a quote from Charley Gant: "The Ladies Social Club deserves great credit for the efforts being put forth to secure for the people on the island a public hall. No body of women anywhere, with no greater opportunity, has done more to advance socially and morally the community in which they live.

The club didn't always run smoothly, though. At one point the vice president was ejected from the club because she was neglectful of her duties, and guilty of harmful gossip. She accused the club president of using club money when she had no right. There were also other ladies forced to resign over a period of time. There was even a time when there was talk of deeding the property back to Mr. Kidd. But at the January meeting in 1914, it was recommended that a hall 30 x 60, with a smoking room upstairs, be built. They borrowed $300 from Jack Kidd, who had already donated the land. The men cut and piled the brush on that piece of property, and the women burned it. Then a crew of men, headed by C.H. Dunn, went to work on the building and finished it in March 1914. There was a dedication, of course, with speeches and a social.

The first big dance was held April 15, 1914. The couples from across the channel paid $1.00 per couple. The islanders paid fifty cents per couple because they furnished the refreshments and did all the work. The sum of $94.90 was received from the dance, with 10 cents found on the floor, making it an even $95.00! From then on dances were given and attended regularly at the hall.

It was October 1914 when men were invited to join the Social Club, and fifteen of them did. After that the men took over the dances. They also formed an athletic club and a basketball team.

In January 1915, the hall and property were deeded to the trustees of the Booster Club in trust for the island people.

The Social Club was still meeting in February, 1916, but there are no records after that. It should be mentioned that the ladies of that organization made two U.S. flags - one for the new hall, and one for Charley Gant's office. They also contributed money towards two shed-barns, one on each side of the ferry dock, to hold the teams and horses while their owners went across the channel.

Volunteering - both financially and with labor - has been

part of and contributed to the growth of Guemes since the beginning.

Here are a few examples.

The schoolhouse was built in 1885 on an acre of ground donated by William Eden. A contribution of $160.00 was made from public school funds. The remainder of the money, and the labor, were donated by the people on the island. When the building was finished, more money was needed, and was given, for desks and seats. The building, by the way, was also used for such island activities as church, meetings, dances and parties.

The cemetery deed was executed in 1904; the land donated by the Edens. The gate columns were erected in 1934. The money for this project was raised by subscription, and the labor done by volunteers. More cemetery land was also donated by Henry Howard and William Payne.

In 1912, one of the first jobs of the newly-formed Improvement and Booster Club was the clearing of the road for rural mail delivery. Also, that spring they cleared the school yard so as to make a larger play area for the children. At that time there were 42 children in the school.

In 1913, the club raised $152.00 toward building a more substantial ferry dock. They also slashed the road from the ferry dock to the schoolhouse, making it straighter and widening it to 50 feet. Property owners on each side of the road donated enough property to make this possible. Even as late as 1918, the residents were donating labor and money for new roads.

A great deal of volunteer labor and money have gone into the little church too - from the beginning up to the present time. It started when the Ladies Aid raised $40.00 to buy the one half acre of land. Gertrude Magill even asked the merchants in town for donations to help build the church.

In 1955, sixty-two of the island residents contributed $305.00 towards drilling the well, the pump, etc. Volunteer labor dug the ditch for the pipe from the hall to the church. It was 1958 when the "powder room" was added.

In 1964, the hall underwent extensive remodeling. Some of the labor was hired and paid for, but there was also much volunteer help. It was a time of a new roof, new foundation and a new floor. The stage was removed and a furnace installed. The memorial funds of H.W. Whicker and Lage Wernstedt, supplemented by the club, were used for renovation and remodeling of the kitchen. In 1965, the memorial fund for Bob Howard was used to buy the light fixtures in the hall. The siding was put on and painted in 1966.

Volunteer labor was also used to build the fire hall. That was in 1963. That property was bought from Dot Graham. A class for the volunteer firemen was conducted in 1964 by the State Vocational Training Program. It was a six-week course, and each week the women took turns, in groups of three, preparing hot lunches for the men.

The ferry tale could be turned into a large volume - maybe two. And most people know the ongoing story.

Rowing, of course, was the popular mode of transportation for the settlers. Most owned a canoe or rowboat. However, steamers stopped fairly regularly on Guemes in the early 1870's for passengers, mail and freight. These steamers also picked up wood for fuel for their vessels which some of the pioneers cut and sold for $1.75 per cord.

The first mention I have been able to find of a ferry to Guemes was in the 1890 paper. The small notice said: "W.C Pyle, our genial ferryman is chuckfull of good nature and accommodation. When you wish to cross over to Guemes fail not to call on ferryman Pyle." About 1910, there were two small passenger-carrying boats - one called Sunny Jim and the other, Glide.

In 1912, a launch named Elk was put into passenger service to and from Guemes. This boat was owned and skippered by Harry Rickaby, who had come west from New Jersey in 1882. The Elk made six trips daily. The contract Was given by the county at $105.00 per month, and the fare was five cents each way. The boat carried 35 passengers. Frank Taylor, Don Taylor's father, was in partnership with Mr. Rickaby for a time. By 1916, Mr. Rickaby also offered "Scow and Freight Service, and Excursions and Picnic Parties anywhere, at any time."

That year Charley Gant wrote: "There may come a time when the county will give us a free ferry to Guemes, but that time is not now. And there may come a time when the county will give us no ferry at all. The slogan of the settlers of Guemes and the merchants of Anacortes has been: A five cent ferry making five trips daily. We have secured a five-cent ferry making six trips daily, and it is the best service Guemes has ever had."

The ferry Guemes was built in 1917 for a private group who called themselves Guemes Ferry Co., Inc. Bill Bessner bought the boat January 1, 1922, and ran it for 28 years. The Guemes changed hands twice more before the Almar replaced it. The Almar made its first official landing on Guemes at 1:00 p.m., January 5, 1960. The county bought the ferry in 1963 for $36,000. An item of interest: from 1955 through 1969, Sandy Bernsen received a $775.00 monthly subsidy from the county for county trucks and equipment, and for the school children.

Bits and Pieces at Random

The first school on the island was built in 1873. It was a log building located about 3/4 of a mile from the present ferry landing - a short distance in back of the half-torn-down little cabin east of the now Pat Palmer place. The school at the cross-roads, as I've said before, was built in 1885. Guemes residents voted for school consolidation in 1948. At that time, children through the 4th grade were kept on the island - the remainder were bussed to the Anacortes schools. The Guemes school was closed in 1962.

* *

The Indian children were sent to the Chemewa Indian School near Salem, Oregon. This is where Sarah and George Kingston first met. George didn't like it at the school, so he ran away and came home. Mary Merchant and the older Blackinton children were also among the children who went to that school.

* *

Mary Merchant showed me an interesting Abstract of Title once. It was homestead certificate #1295 granting 158-90/100 acres to Luscius Blackinton in January 1882, and signed by President Chester A. Arthur. In 1888, aster changing hands at least two times, the land was sold to Cyrus Clapp who platted the town of Guemes by laying off the land into lots, blocks and streets. In 1906 the county commissioners were petitioned for vacation of the plat—and it was vacated. Part of the sound side—east of the ferry dock—was also platted into town lots. This happened in 1889, and was named North Anacortes.

* *

The first rural mail delivery was in 1913. In the beginning, the mail was taken back and forth in a rowboat. Some of the famil-iar names among the Guemes mail carriers were: Herb Caus-land, Robin Gould and George Pinneo. Our present postmaster, Lavern Deane, was also once a Guemes carrier. The delivery was done first on foot, then by horseback, then by horse and cart, until the auto finally arrived on the scene.

* *

In 1914 the population on Guemes was about 300, and there were 30 children in school.

* *

Sarah Kingston seemed to think the winters were colder when she was young. She remembered that the ponds were frozen over and that nearly everyone skated and had skating parties.
Shrimp fishing in the channel was profitable about 1912. The Guemes residents would row out to the shrimp boats and buy fresh shrimp.

* *

During World War I, soldiers were stationed on Guemes in barracks on the south slope of the island.

* *

Cooks Bay was named for E.S. Cook, a wealthy and prominent business man who owned that property and had quite an estate there - two houses, barns and other outbuildings, and also a swimming pool. Fred and Jennie Pinneo became caretakers of Bonnie Brae, as Mr. Cook had named it and, while there, sold water from the springs on the place to the Ice Company in town for use in making pop. They rowed across the channel with the water in milk cans - about 50 gallons each time. The end to that enterprise came when they were caught in a strong westerly coming back to the island, and the boat crashed against the rocks on the beach and was damaged beyond repair. When the Pinneos wanted to cross on the ferry they would first have to row from Cooks Bay. There were no through roads at that time.

Another Jennie Pinneo story: when she and Fred moved to the Cook place, Jennie had her piano moved over. The men who brought it in a boat or scow, unloaded it on the beach and left. The piano sat there all night - fortunately above high tide - until the Pinneos could get help to move it the next day.

* *

The first 4th of July celebration on the island was held in 1876 at the Wilfong place, which was on South Beach in the area where the Mills now live. The first 4th of July parade was held on North Beach in 1938.

The first telephone service was in 1908 when a 3,450 foot cable was laid across the channel.

Electricity became a reality in 1949.

The first community Thanksgiving was held in the hall in 1914.

Our road signs were put up in 1960, and garbage service was started that same year.

Potluck suppers were started on a permanent basis at community club meetings in 1953.

Until 1955 the hall was heated by a large pot-bellied stove.

The Country Store at the Salmon Barbecue began in 1958.

Frank Taylor told me about a stern wheeler - a passenger and freight vessel - that caught fire at the city dock about 19 11. It was cut free and floated across the channel to a point near the now Donnelly place, where it, sank.

* *

A proposal for Guemes in 1950 was a Federal Government experimental station for hoof and mouth disease. And in 1954 the state was looking for a site for a corrective school for boys 10 to 14 years of age to relieve the congestion at Chehalis. Senator Luvera suggested

Guemes Island. Neither proposal, of course, materialized.

* *

The rafters in the first fire hall came from the old barn on the old Frank Lopp place, and were donated by Wade Gilkey. That barn was located on the farm where Jeff Winston now lives.

* *

In 1948 there were 135 houses on the island and 76 mail boxes.

* *

The assessed valuation of Guemes Island in 1950 was $96,265.00 and now, in 1980, it is $20,073,983.00.

* *

In 1921 William Kager (the present Kager's grandfather) settled on West Beach. He drained the swamp or pond there, and planted wheat, had a truck garden and a turkey farm. At that time there were only two houses on that beach, and the road ran in front of those houses along the beach.

* *

The P.T.A. turned the salmon barbecue over to the Community Club in 1955, the amount taken in was $49.80.

* *

Charles Stapp, one of our long-time, hard-working islanders, was chairman of the Park Committee in Anacortes when it was decided, in 1919, that Mr. LePage should build the rock work at Causland Park. And, of course, the park was named for another islander, Harry Causland, who was a World War I hero.

* *

William Lowman planted the cherry orchard - 1,000 trees about 1910.

* *

Land values have changed over the years. Here is an ad that appeared in the "Tillikum" in 1913.

> "56 acre ranch on Guemes Island, 25 acres under cultivation, team, wagon, buggy, harness, farming implements, 6 milch cows, 2 calves, pigs, cream separator, new 7-room house, barn 30 x 50, young orchard, small fruit, 500 cords of shingle bolts (238 cords cut). This is waterfront property. Price: $5,000. 00."

And in 1923 - "5-room cottage, 1 acre of land - $900.00.

Also in 1921 -- The shipyard property was sold to a Tacoma man who dismantled the buildings and removed all traces of the Guemes industry that had been built in 1917. The total property, including 28 acres, was sold for $6,000.00.

* *

A verse from one of Charley Gant's poems:

"I don't want to go out to encounter gales
On waters uncharted, unknown
Where here I can follow the calm, love-lit trails
With friends and not travel alone.
I want to stay here where the gorgeous dyes
Of the rainbows can ever be found
Over ever blue seas, under ever blue skies
In the ever Green Land of Puget Sound."

Made in the USA
Charleston, SC
08 March 2011